Speakers! The Quick Public Speaking to Business Method™

Ellen Finkelstein

and

Connie Ragen Green

ISBN Paperback: 978-1-937988-53-1
ISBN eBook: 978-1-937988-54-8

Hunter's Moon Publishing
http://HuntersMoonPublishing.com

Hunter's Moon Publishing - Connie Ragen Green
P.O. Box 3295
Santa Barbara, CA 93130-3295

Ellen Finkelstein - ChangetheWorldMarketing.com
Connie Ragen Green - ConnieRagenGreen.com

Limits of Liability and Disclaimer of Warranty

Warning - Disclaimer

As the purchaser of this book we (Connie Ragen Green and Ellen Finkelstein) wish to gift you ongoing resources designed to assist you in your journey to creating an ongoing revenue stream with your public speaking. Opt in to receive our complimentary Resources for Speakers at: https://OnlineWritingProfits.com/speaker-resources

This training will assist you along your speaking journey.

What People Are Saying

"People tend to fall into two categories. Some seek out knowledge and experiences and then file them away in the back of their minds. Then, there are others who not only seek greater knowledge and deeper experiences but also take it much further. They choose to embrace what they have learned and use it in their daily lives to enhance their life experience and to help others do the same. You may have guessed that Connie is someone who does the latter. I am one of many people who has benefitted from this enlightened style of thinking and belief system."

~ Joann Waldman

"Every now and then you find someone with the perfect balance of skill, knowledge and passion for what they do. You find those qualities in Ellen Finkelstein. Her expertise in book writing has made a huge difference in my life. I have no qualms in recommending Ellen to anyone who want to grow their business."

~ Ron Price

Opt In to Receive Our Complimentary Resources for Speakers at:
https://OnlineWritingProfits.com/speaker-resources

This training will assist you along your speaking journey.

Table of Contents

Dedication

This book is dedicated to all of the people we (Ellen Finkelstein and Connie Ragen Green) have worked with over the years who yearn for a platform to share their message with the world. Our goal is to guide you closer to finding a way to make that happen. We have encouraged you and guided you along this path. Now we have written this book so that you may continue to create an ongoing stream of revenue by speaking.

You have been a public speaker since you first shared your story aloud and captured someone's attention. That someone was most likely a parent, sibling, or other family member and you were probably a toddler or preschooler at the time. The endorphins released in that moment shifted your brain chemistry and shaped you into the person you were in the process of becoming. Now you have arrived and your true journey is about to begin.

May your words reach the people who most need to hear your message, all around the world and in a way that motivates and inspires them to move mountains and change lives.

Speakers! The Quick Public Speaking to Business Method™

Turning Your Talk into an Ongoing Revenue Stream

Ellen Finkelstein

&

Connie Ragen Green

Foreword

It was a cold and windy night in Cellular Field, home of the Chicago White Sox. Connie Ragen Green and I were huddled under a blanket with other members of our mastermind group, watching the game and trying not to freeze while watching the baseball game.

That's the weekend that we first met face-to-face in March 2009 - and we've been friends and colleagues ever since. It was while waiting for our flights home in the Concierge Lounge at O'Hare International Airport that we decided to do a project together.

That project became "Dotcom Jump Start" which we launched in July. By the following January we were hosting our first 3-day workshop in Las Vegas. And the rest is history.

When we first started working together Connie failed to mention that she didn't know how to create a PowerPoint presentation. But after I received her 200-slide stack, which I reformatted into 30 slides, I began to understand. She was always willing to try, to learn, to improve, to strive to be and do her best.

That's the attitude that she brings to everything she does. Approach it with enthusiasm. Do the best you can. Learn from it. Repeat.

I had only recently found out she wasn't an experienced speaker when we hosted that first conference. Instead, she prepared, watched other speakers, improved and pulled it off like a pro! After all, in her prior life she had been a classroom teacher, talking to kids and parents. She was a realtor, talking to clients and community groups. This was just like that - but it may feel different when you're in front of an audience paying to learn from you.

In the past 15 years I've watched Connie perfect her skills while becoming one of the favorite speakers in the markets with whom she works. Her ready humor and willingness to learn make her an enjoyable speaker on stage or in small groups.

She has also learned the business side of speaking. As a 20-year veteran of the National Speakers Association, I can tell you that that is the difference between giving a speech and speaking profitably. And that's one of the focuses of this book - using speaking as a revenue stream or to build your other revenue streams.

Ellen comes from a different background. We met several years ago working on a project for authors after she already had a well-established business. We both come from a speaking background. We both love PowerPoint - in fact, Ellen is an established expert in the field, consulting and speaking for top companies. She has published numerous books and articles, as well as spoken profitably for years. Ellen has followed the model in this book quite successfully!

In short, you could not have found two better qualified people to share these steps with you.

Regardless of your background, your perceived speaking skills, or your business model - you will learn from this book. I highly recommend these two experts and I know you will enjoy the experience. Go, learn, speak, profit. Repeat.

Jeanette S. Cates, PhD

Author & 20-year member of the National Speakers Association

Austin, TX

November, 2020

Preface

This book came about as a response to the many questions we (Ellen and Connie) have received from people in our vast communities who are interested in adding the speaking model to their business.

It makes sense that people who write and teach on their topics would also become known and successful as public speakers. And as successful entrepreneurs, authors, and speakers in our own right, we also want this lifestyle for you.

From Connie Ragen Green:

I didn't want to become a public speaker. I was afraid to speak to even a small group of people from the time I was a little girl. Just the thought of speaking to people I knew, let alone to those I did not know scared me to the point that I would get nauseous and dizzy and my mouth would become as dry as the Sahara Desert.

It wasn't until the eighth grade that I was forced to participate in a one-semester class on speaking. I struggled through each week, and it was only when the assignment called for us to teach the others students something that I was able to get through my talk more easily. I showed them how to make Christmas ornaments out of the pointy cardboard egg cartons we got at the local Publix market and even the boys had fun making them.

Another decade or so and I found it advantageous to speak once in a while as part of my work in real estate. I served snacks and that distracted most everyone until my Lunch 'n Learn presentation was over. Ten years later and I was speaking to my students in the classroom, but that didn't feel like public speaking and I enjoyed it. Two more decades and I wanted to start a business.

Everyone told me speaking would open doors. It would also help me with visibility and credibility. I resisted until I could not deny that everyone was right. I looked for inspiration and found it in two quotes from former First Lady Eleanor Roosevelt. She is known for saying two things that speak directly to me. They are:

"You must do the thing you think you cannot do" and "Do one thing every day that scares you."

Both of these, for me are public speaking. It was the one thing I believed I could not do. And just the thought of speaking scared me. So, I did it anyway; I chose to speak in spite of these perceived obstacles.

The process was painful in the beginning but I challenged myself to do more speaking. When I spoke, I was doing the thing I thought I could not do, even if it was physically discomforting. And after a few times I wasn't scared any longer.

Many doors and opportunities soon opened to me and these days it's difficult to get a microphone out of my hands once I have it. Now I'm looking for more things I think I cannot do that will scare me every day. The adventure continues...

It was 2006 and I had just arrived in my new city. After resigning my job as a classroom teacher at the end of the school year, as well as giving away my best real estate clients to others who could better serve them, I decided to relocate as part of my life reinvention. I was ready to start my new business on the internet. Within a couple of weeks, I came to the realization that working from home was going to be a lonely proposition.

This led to a search for volunteer opportunities in my new community. The international service organization Rotary held weekly meetings and I showed up to see what it was all about. Soon they asked me to do a talk about this new internet business I had been telling them about. I was scared to death but knew they were supportive of my endeavors and wanted to do more. On that hot and humid day in August of 2006, my speaking career was launched in front of sixty Rotarians at the Marie Callendar's restaurant.

Soon after I was invited for speaking engagements for the local Chamber of Commerce and the Rotary District event with more than three hundred in attendance. I was still so scared each time I got up on stage and prayed for the confidence to be able to speak in front of groups of any size. It would be a full two years before that occurred.

It was in Minneapolis, Minnesota in June of 2008 and I had been asked by legendary marketer Armand Morin to speak at his annual event. I passed him in the hallway on my way to the conference room and he asked me if I was nervous. I nodded yes, but shared with him that I was not as nervous as I had been previously when speaking.

When I got up on stage the nerves crept back in and I assumed this would be another time where my mouth would get dry and I would read most of the slides, making very little eye contact with anyone in the audience.

But something happened that I cannot explain. It began when I said something funny and a few people laughed. Then I said something else and I was building rapport with the group. I sailed through my presentation, interacted by answering a few questions, and sold several copies of the program I was offering.

In those moments I told myself to remember how this felt. I had wanted this feeling and experience so badly and now I knew I could call myself a public speaker and change my life forever.

These days I speak virtually and in person on a regular basis. Sharing my message with others is a gift for which I will be eternally grateful.

Doing the thing I thought I could not do continues to change my life.

From Ellen Finkelstein:

In my last year of college, I did something that must have freaked out my parents, although they didn't let on. I withdrew from college to go to a course to become a teacher of the Transcendental Meditation™ program. (When I got back, I finished the credits I needed and graduated.)

For the next few years, I gave introductory lectures on TM. I felt passionate about the topic and the audience was usually small, so I didn't feel too nervous. On the other hand, I hadn't done anything to become a good speaker and shudder to think how I might have looked and sounded.

That ended in 1977 or so, when I took a job as a Benefits Assistant and then another as a Benefits Manager. I did a small amount of speaking in-house, explaining benefits to new employees and explaining new benefits to all existing employees. I was the expert and that didn't feel scary because it was all within the company.

I started my at-home career when my children were very young, so I could be at home with them. First, I did technical editing for IDG Books, which became Wiley & Sons. Then, I got my first opportunity to write a book on AutoCAD, a computer drafting program. It was a stroke of luck – the intended author could no longer fulfill his obligations to write the book and the publisher knew me because of my work as a technical editor on that topic.

That started a long career writing computer books, including one book on AutoCAD that went for 17 editions and was translated into 14 languages – and ended up being 1,200 pages!

During that time, I had the opportunity to create test questions and answers for a textbook on PowerPoint. By reading the text and creating the questions and answers, I learned PowerPoint. I continued to write several books on PowerPoint for McGraw-Hill's Osborne division.

To create a platform for my books, I started ellenfinkelstein.com in 1999. I blogged regularly on both AutoCAD and PowerPoint. It was an odd combination, but the overlap was that they both involved graphics. I built up a list of email subscribers, many of whom are still getting my newsletters, years later.

Then, a company that sold webinars to businesses asked me to do a webinar for them. I still remember my first one – it was SO strange speaking to people I couldn't see! But I just went through it. Apparently, it went well because they asked me back and I did a number of these for a flat fee. It was good practice doing the webinars but not having to deal with the webinar platform or the promotion. After 2 years, I got up the nerve to organize my own webinars. I mostly spoke about PowerPoint and presenting.

As I developed my online business, I also spoke at a couple of Internet marketing conferences and found that to be fun – but I realized that I needed to improve my speaking skills.

I enrolled in the local Toastmasters group. My first impromptu 2-minute talk was scary! I still remember feeling my heart pounding in my chest, but again I pushed through it. Over the next few months, I completed my Competent Communication designation. I recommend Toastmasters for every new speaker. You'll get a fair amount of short-format practice with supportive, constructive feedback.

In 2010, I created the Outstanding Presentations Workshop, a web summit with a series of experts speaking about presenting, with myself as the last speaker. This had a huge effect on my reputation as a presentation speaker, because I was associated with the other experts. I've organized it each year since then. In the second year, when it was still free, we had just over 3,000 registrants from 97 countries.

It's SO rewarding to be able to reach so many people from all around the world! You can do something similar!

Since then, I've spoken on stages and online and I must say that I prefer speaking online. I can reach more people with less travel.

Because I'm not naturally a smooth speaker, I've challenged myself to speak extemporaneously as much as possible. I do a very short Facebook Live with no script 4-5 days per week for my membership program members and a slightly longer one once a week for my public Change the World Marketing Facebook group, with just a few points to go from.

I strongly recommend practicing this type of speaking. Facebook Lives are an idea way to do this. Once you have this skill, it's with you for life.

Speaking, including speaking about speaking – and now, writing about speaking – has been transformational for me personally and professionally.

Introduction

We are excited for you as you embark upon your journey of public speaking as an income stream and an integral part of your business. You will have within you the power to educate, inform, and change the hearts and minds of the people with whom you share your message. Whether you are speaking virtually or in person you will experience the shift that occurs when someone hears what you have to say. Your words will land on them and set afloat their dreams of doing something differently in their life.

In the first part of this book, we discuss Speaking as a Business Model. This includes learning about the history of speaking so that we have a foundation on which to build. We then move on to other speakers who have used the speaking to income model successfully over time and up to the present day. Then you will learn how to choose a topic that is right for you. Finally, you will understand how to define your goals as a speaker so you can stay on track and act purposefully with your speaking business.

Part II takes us to Turning Your Speaking into a Business. In Chapter 6, we talk about the importance of relationships. This chapter also includes an interview with Rebecca Morgan., a highly successful speaker and consultant in the field of leadership.

Chapter 7, The Art and Science of the Funnel, explains the process of using your speech to make a free offer to get subscribers so that you can sell them products and services.

The many ways to create relationships via email is covered in Chapter 8.

Chapter 9 is about developing your business on your website and creating a selling platform for your products and services.

In the final chapter in this section, Chapter 10, we explain how to use social media to grow your business—and how to use social media strategically without wasting time.

This is followed by Part III, where we discuss Moving Forward with Speaking as an Income Stream. This includes tips and strategies for putting yourself out there, procuring speaking engagements, delivering your talk in person, asking "What's for Sale?" and selling from the stage.

We share the powerful art of storytelling in Part IV. This includes using your story in every aspect of your speaking and business, speaking to inspire and persuade, and crafting a signature speech.

Part V ends the book to inspire you to take the next steps necessary for you to turn your speaking into income.

Your speaking empowers you, as well as the people who are fortunate enough to hear you speak. Be willing to take the necessary steps from where you are today as a speaker to closer to where you would like to be with your speaking to turn your talk into an ongoing revenue stream. We are here to support you with your efforts and look forward to further connecting with you.

Part I
Speaking as a Business Model

*"If you don't know where you are going,
any road will take you there."
~ Lewis Carroll*

In this first section we will lay the groundwork and introduce you to some basic concepts about the world of public speaking. This is a magical world where anything and everything is possible and lives are shaped and transformed in the process.

Knowing the history of an area you will be incorporating into your life in a major way gives you insight into what came before. It is only through the study of the historical background of speaking and speakers that we can grow and help to change the future of public speaking as communication and a business model.

Then we will take a look at other speakers who have used their platform to create an income stream. Emulating those speakers who have motivated and inspired you over the years and continue to do so gives you a perspective rooted in knowledge, emotions, and results so that you will have a bird's eye view of the outcomes you are seeking.

Choosing your topic of influence will guide you to achieving the goals you have set for yourself as you refine your speaking over time. This will make a difference in how you approach each speech and speaking assignment along the way.

Defining your goals as a speaker will enable you to forge a path that is both enjoyable and logical. If we don't know where we're going, we are likely to end up somewhere else far off the original path we were seeking. There are several models that we will share and elaborate on for more clarity.

We move on to the importance of preparing your speech well in advance and crafting it in such a way that it flows naturally as you are delivering it to your audience.

Let's get started...

Chapter One

The History of Speaking

"We are not the makers of history. We are made by history."
~ Dr. Martin Luther King, Jr.

It is important, I believe, to understand and review the history of speaking and oration before we delve into the modern world of public speaking, and of speaking as a business model. Our current knowledge and practice of public speaking in the 21st Century draws upon ancient Greek, Roman, and Western thought.

Speaking was the earliest form of communication between human beings. Whether it was cavemen and women grunting and gesturing and uttering guttural sounds, or the first word that could be distinguished from all the others, voiced speech has been with us since humans first roamed the earth.

According to my research, the first word ever shared out loud with another human was "Aa," which meant "Hey!" This was said by an australopithecine in Ethiopia more than a million years ago; (Australopithecine are defined as any of the various extinct hominids (genera Australopithecus and Paranthropus) that existed two to four million years ago in southern and eastern Africa).

Some of the oldest forms of human communication include talking or making sounds and hand gestures and body movement, leading into stories and other memories passed down by the elders of the tribe or village.

Making the transition between talking and speaking wasn't as big a leap as you might imagine. Both are common modes of communication and it makes sense that some people would choose to impart their thoughts, ideas, and experiences to others in a way that would be the forerunner to modern public speaking.

But let's first step back in history to biblical times. Now I am not a biblical scholar, so please bear with me in my attempt at oversimplifying what I am discussing with you here. My goal is to share the history of speaking with you in a way that might pique your interest or curiosity on this topic.

You may be familiar with John 1:1 in the Bible where it says, "In the beginning was the Word, and the Word was with God, and the Word was God."

I longed to know what *the word* was and what it meant, so I engaged in some relevant research. What I discovered is fascinating, especially if you are gearing up for a life of public speaking on one or more topics.

The Greek translation of *word* is logos, meaning word, message, or report. When someone is speaking, they are sharing a message with those who are listening to what is being said.

The word oration is from the Latin, with *orare* meaning speak or pray and *oratio* translating as discourse or prayer. It makes sense that the idea of speaking in public is tied so closely with religious and spiritual themes. Public speaking (also called oratory or oration) is the process or act of performing a speech to a live audience. An oration speech is a formal speech that is given on a special occasion. For example, oration speeches are often made at a school commencement exercise or a presidential inauguration.

Public speaking is commonly understood as formal, face-to-face speaking of a single person to a group of listeners. Traditionally, public speaking was considered to be a part of the art of persuasion. The act of speaking to others can accomplish some particular purposes including to inform, to persuade, and to entertain. Public speaking can serve the purpose of transferring information, sharing a story, motivating people to act in a certain way. Or encouraging people to think and take action. Knowing when public speaking is most effective and how it is done properly are key to understanding the importance of it.

Additionally, differing methods, structures, and rules can be utilized according to the specific speaking situation. We will discuss each of these in great detail throughout this book.

Speaking as a Vocation Began in Ancient Rome and Greece

It was in ancient Rome and Greece that public speaking was first developed as a vocation. Prominent thinkers from these areas influenced the development and evolutionary history of public speaking. Their work so long ago continues to affect us today, and technology continues to transform the art of public speaking through newly available innovation such as webinars, videoconferencing, multimedia presentations, and other nontraditional forms.

Today's professionals are often responsible for the public speaking for business and commercial events. This began in ancient Rome and Greece, where teachers, lawyers, and doctors were expected to share their beliefs and findings with the general populous. In today's world, these speakers can be contracted independently, through representation by a speaker's bureau, or by other means. Public speaking plays a large role in the professional world. In fact, it is believed that at least 70 percent of all jobs involve some form of public speaking. Later in the book I'll discuss in greater detail what it is like to be at a job or in a career that requires you to speak publicly, sometimes putting yourself in the public eye in the process.

Great Orators from Ancient Times

The formal study of public speaking began approximately 2,500 years ago in Greece and Rome to train citizens to participate in society. The educated person (almost exclusively men at this time in our history) guided the masses with their thoughts, beliefs, and ideas turned into words. Aristotle (384-322 BCE) is the most famous Greek Scholar and influenced every type and style of speaking that has come to be known since that time.

Aristotle was one of the first recorded teachers of oratory to use definitive rules and models with his pupils. His emphasis on oratory led to oration becoming an essential part of a liberal arts education during the Middle Ages and throughout the Renaissance. The classical antiquity works written by the ancient Greeks capture the ways they taught and developed the art of public speaking thousands of years ago.

He studied in Plato's Academy where he later taught public speaking until Plato's death in 347 BCE. During this time, Aristotle opened his own school of politics, science, philosophy, and rhetoric.

What Do We Mean by "Rhetoric"?

Aristotle defined rhetoric as "the faculty of observing in any given case the available means of persuasion" and since mastery of the art was necessary for victory in a case at law; or for passage of proposals in the assembly; or for fame as a speaker in civic ceremonies; he calls it "a combination of the science of logic and of the ethical branch of politics." Rhetoric typically provides heuristics for understanding, discovering, and developing arguments for particular situations, such as Aristotle's three persuasive audience appeals: logos, pathos, and ethos. The five canons of rhetoric or phases of developing a persuasive speech were first codified in classical Rome: invention, arrangement, style, memory, and delivery.

Rhetoric, classically the theoretical basis for the art of oratory, is the art of using words effectively. Oratory is instrumental and practical, as distinguished from poetic or literary composition, which traditionally aims at beauty and pleasure. Oratory is of the marketplace and as such not always concerned with the universal and permanent. The orator in his purpose and technique is primarily persuasive rather than informational or entertaining. An attempt is made to change human behavior or to strengthen convictions and attitudes. The orator would correct wrong positions of the audience and establish psychological patterns favorable to his own wishes and platform. Argument and rhetorical devices are used, as are evidence, lines of reasoning, and appeals that support the orator's aims. Exposition is employed to clarify and enforce the orator's propositions, and anecdotes and illustrations are used to heighten response.

Rhetoric is the art of persuasion, which along with grammar and logic, is one of the three ancient arts of discourse. Rhetoric aims to study the capacities of writers or speakers needed to inform, persuade, or motivate particular audiences in specific situations.

From Ancient Greece to the late 19th century, rhetoric played a central role in Western education in training orators, lawyers, teachers, historians, statesmen, and poets.

We simply cannot discuss the work of Aristotle without going back even further in time.

Rhetoric During the Classical Period (500 BCE – 400 BCE)

The ancient Greeks highly valued public political participation, where public speaking was a crucial tool. In addition to Aristotle, the thought leaders in this area included the Greek philosophers Aspasia of Miletus, Socrates, and Plato.

Aspasia of Miletus (469 BCE), the "mother of rhetoric," is believed to have been the philosopher who taught rhetoric to Socrates. During this period Pericles, the Athenian ruler and Aspasia's partner, treated Aspasia as an equal and allowed her the opportunity to engage in dialogue with the important and educated men of society.

Socrates (469-399 BCE) greatly influenced the direction of the Classical Period. Most of what we know about Socrates comes from the writings of his student, Plato.

Plato (429-347 BCE) wrote about rhetoric in the form of dialogues with Socrates as the main character. Plato defined the scope of rhetoric according to his negative opinions of the art. He criticized the Sophists for using rhetoric as a means of deceit instead of discovering truth.

Oratory is the rationale and practice of persuasive public speaking. It is immediate in its audience relationships and reactions, but it may also have broad historical repercussions. The orator may become the voice of political or social history.

An excellent example of the way a speech can focus the concerns of a nation was Martin Luther King's address to a massive civil rights demonstration in Washington, D.C., in 1963. Repeating the phrase "I have a dream," King applied the oratorical skill he had mastered as a preacher to heighten his appeal to the United States government and its citizens for further rights for Black Americans to an intensity that galvanized millions and brought about the most significant change of circumstances in more than five hundred years.

An oration involves a speaker; an audience; a background of time, place, and other conditions; a message; transmission by voice, articulation, and bodily accompaniments; and may, or may not, have an immediate outcome.

Now that you have a deeper understanding of the history of public speaking and oration, and of how rhetoric became crucial to the art of persuasion in modern times, let's discuss the speakers who have emerged as ones who use this as their business model.

CHAPTER TWO

Speakers Who Use This Model

"The purpose of speaking is to create a change in people
and to move them to take action.
You want to make the world a better place.
Maybe not the entire world at once,
maybe just one person at a time."
~ Ellen Finkelstein

I would like for you to think back over the years to speakers you have heard, either in person at a conference or theatrical performance, on television or radio, or virtually over the internet. Who comes to mind? What made them memorable to you? Think about the people who moved you to action and a shift in your thinking with their inspiring and motivating speeches. What action, if any, did you take soon after hearing their message?

During the late summer of 1995 I attended a marketing conference in Los Angeles. I had been invited by a friend with whom I was seldom able to spend much time with in person. I only agreed to go so that I could spend the day visiting with my friend and also to get away from my usual routine. This was long before I understood the value and importance of making a study of marketing. Little did I know that attending this event would shift my thinking and plant the seed for a major life change over the next several years.

It wouldn't be an exaggeration for me to say that what occurred on that day was a precursor to my resigning from my teaching position and giving away my best real estate clients to start my online business eleven years later.

There were several speakers that day, and to be honest I can't name them all any longer. But when Les Brown took the stage my life would be changed forever. The emcee introduced him and I watched his facial expression and body movements as he crossed the stage and arrived at the podium. Before Les had uttered a word, I felt like I already knew him. It was something about the way he walked that told me this man had led a challenging life. Something in the way he moved his arms and tilted his head, slightly to the left told me he was an excellent listener. And something in the way he stood slightly to the right of the podium and looked out over the audience told me he cared deeply about people and would do whatever was possible to share information with us on that day that would make a difference in our lives.

Can you imagine someone having that kind of impact on you, before they've uttered a single word? That's exactly the effect Les Brown had on me, and this is the power you can have as a public speaker. But even if you are able to affect your audience in that way, it must be followed up with a solid message and some solid and proven strategies. This is so the people you are speaking to will have a way to experience what you're teaching for themselves.

This process is most effectively done through an offer you will sell at the end of your talk, and one you have been leading up to for some time while you are on stage. I'm getting way ahead of myself here, but please know that Ellen and I will be sharing everything we know, both individually and collectively with you throughout this book.

In the case of Les Brown, he began to introduce us to who he was and what he stood for by sharing a story of his early life in south Florida. I had lived in Miami as a teenager and knew from my firsthand experience that the area of town he grew up in was a rough one for people of any age, let alone for young children.

Leslie Calvin Brown and his twin brother, Wesley, were born on February 17, 1945, on the second floor of an abandoned building in Liberty City, a low-income and crime ridden section of Miami. Their birth mother, married at the time to a soldier stationed overseas, had become pregnant by another man and went to Miami during her final months of pregnancy to give birth to her sons. Three weeks later, she gave them up for adoption and left town so as not to get the word out on what had happened. They were placed in a Catholic orphanage after leaving the hospital.

At six weeks of age, both boys were adopted by Mamie Brown, a 38-year-old single woman who worked as a cafeteria cook and housekeeper. She had been unable to have children of her own and this was the blessing she had prayed for over many years. Les considered his mother a key influence in his life, telling Rachel L. Jones of the Detroit Free Press, "Everything I am and everything I have I owe to my mother. Her strength and character are my greatest inspiration, always have been and always will be."

As a child, Brown was considered to be hyperactive and mischievous. He struggled in school, finding it impossible to concentrate, and in the 5th grade was designated as being "educable mentally retarded" and taken out of the regular classroom. It was a label he found hard to remove, in large part because he did not try. "They said I was slow so I held to that pace," he recounted.

However, a dedicated teacher saw greater potential. LeRoy Washington, a speech and drama instructor at Booker T. Washington High School in Miami, inspired Les to strive for more. This high school had first opened its doors in 1926 and was the second oldest public high school built for the black residents of Dade County. The school was started by the St. Paul A.M.E. (African Methodist Episcopal) Church and this congregation continues to support its students, alumni, and the community at large.

It was while he was a student at this high school that Brown "used to fantasize being onstage speaking to thousands of people," he related to the journalist, "and I used to write on pieces of paper, 'I am the world's greatest orator'."

When Washington saw potential in Brown, he insisted he live up to it. When Les once told Mr. Washington in class that he couldn't perform a task because he was educable mentally retarded, the instructor vehemently responded, "Do not ever say or think that again! Someone's opinion of you does not have to become your reality."

Those words provided Brown's liberation from his debilitating label. "The limitations you have, and the negative things that you internalize are given to you by the world," he wrote of his realization. "The things that empower you, the possibilities, those come from within." His goal is to deliver a message that will help people become uncomfortable with their mediocrity and that's exactly what happened to me when I heard Les speak on that first day. He shared that a lot of people are content with their discontent. He wanted to be a catalyst to enable them to see themselves having more and achieving more.

By the end of Les' presentation people were already making their way to the tables in the back of the conference room. That is where the event staff was waiting with forms to fill out if you wanted to purchase his course. And, at just the right moment the emcee came on the loudspeaker and told us it was time for a fifteen-minute break. All of this had been carefully orchestrated, as it must be so that Les could receive his well-deserved standing ovation, people could swarm the area in front of the stage to ask him questions, and sales could be made at the back of the room before the next speaker would be introduced.

Even I was excited to purchase a book and an audio recording that day, of Les speaking to another group, and I was probably one of only a few people who had not come to this event with the intention of purchasing anything, especially from someone I hadn't heard of previously. As I was exiting the conference room I glanced back at the stage. Les was still encircled by attendees and his microphone was still on. The last thing I heard him say before the door closed behind me was,

"Be willing to go all out, in pursuit of your dream. Ultimately it will pay off. You are more powerful than you think you are. Go for it."

The door slammed shut behind me and I found myself alone in the hallway. I leaned on the wall to balance my purse and notebook and thought about the speech I had just had the privilege of witnessing and the last words I had heard Les say. In that moment I had a fleeting thought that I would love to be a speaker and share the stage with Les Brown. I repeated his words in my mind and may have even uttered them aloud.

Was I more powerful than I thought I was and could ultimately be? Was I willing to go all out, in pursuit of that dream? Fourteen years later that dream came true and I was a speaker at the same event where Les was speaking. In between sessions I had the chance to speak with him and told him my story. I can still feel his huge arms embracing me and him whispering in my ear, "You are powerful and inspiring and will speak on many stages, sharing your message with others."

Another inspirational speaker who is using the model of speaking to income is Jon Morrow, a professional blogger who came online in 2008 as a way to be taken more seriously as a writer and to help pay for his medical expenses. The wildly successful authority site Copy Blogger brought him aboard and he helped them grow to over three million page views a month, managing dozens of writers and contributing some of the most popular articles on the site. He quickly gained a reputation as being a super smart and talented writer, copywriter, and expert in search engine optimization, as well as someone who valued relationships and building teams to succeed in business. In 2011 Jon decided to branch off from Copy Blogger and launch his own online brand, Smart Blogger, teaching smart, hard-working writers how to get the attention they deserve by starting a blog.

I had already been following Jon for several years when I heard him speak at the *Traffic & Conversion* event in San Diego in 2018. I was attending this annual event with a client of mine, someone who has experienced difficulty with staying focused and following through with the necessary actions to complete his goals.

Throughout the weekend this man had one excuse after another for not writing his book, creating an information product, and blogging regularly. I told him there was someone I wanted him to hear speak and after lunch we met up in the main ballroom of the conference center and chose two seats in the fifth row back from the stage. I remember it was the fifth row because the first four rows had been roped off as the VIP section and it made sense to choose seats as close to the stage as possible.

I hadn't told my client anything about Jon except what was printed in the program regarding his blogging expertise, other than that this next speaker was sure to motivate and inspire him into taking massive action right away. He raised his eyebrows at this but believed I knew of what I was speaking.

Born with a form of muscular dystrophy called Spinal Muscular Atrophy, Jon has spent the vast majority of his adult life almost completely paralyzed, save for being able to move his eyes and lips, which enables him to write through speech recognition technology.

As his wheelchair came into view, and with both his mother and his caretaker close at hand, Jon took the stage to a standing ovation and raucous round of applause and cheers. My client turned to me, took my arm, and whispered, "I believe this will make a difference for me. Thank you."

Jon over delivered that afternoon and I was also inspired in many ways. There is no excuse for not taking action and his message resonated with me and made me want to speak more about my own struggles, challenges, and successes.

There are many people who have used their speaking platform as the basis for building their income. They are from all walks of life and include Seth Godin, Oprah Winfrey, Toni Morrison, Brené Brown, Pamela Slim, and Tim Ferriss, to name just a few speakers that I follow and continue to learn from in this area.

And sometimes it only takes one speech to change people's perception of you. On the evening of January 7th, 2018 Oprah Winfrey took the stage at the Golden Globes awards ceremony to accept the Cecil B. DeMille Award for lifetime achievement. During the next nine minutes Oprah told a story that touched my soul. One line in particular stood out for me:

"What I know for sure is that speaking your truth is the most powerful tool we all have."

Speaking to Share Your Message

Speaking is the way we share what it is in our hearts and minds with those who feel most connected to our message. Think back to a time when you were overcome with joy or grief or any other strong emotion and spoke to others about it. Perhaps it was the high school or college graduation of a family member, making them the first in your family to achieve such a feat. Or perhaps it was the sudden and premature death of a close friend who had so much more life to share and was not able to do so.

I have had both of these life experiences and can remember talking about each of them afterwards, and to multiple people. Now these were not speeches, of course but it was me speaking out loud about the thoughts and feelings that were coming up for me at those times.

Over time you will be able to share your experiences in a meaningful way with audiences of one to one million and every number in between. During the fall of 2011 I auditioned for and was accepted into a professional acting workshop in Los Angeles, California. My goal was to improve my public speaking and to learn how to better share the emotional experiences in my life without breaking down while doing so. The teacher was Fran Montano, a lifelong actor of some renown and a gifted acting teacher.

He agreed to work with me under two conditions. The first of these required my agreeing to stop insisting I didn't want to be an actor; the second was to trust him from the moment each class began until the second we were dismissed. Over my three-month residency in this acting program Fran was able to pull emotions and feelings from me I thought I had long since left behind. I laughed and cried and finally understood what it meant to share a message with my fellow humans.

And by a serendipitous coincidence Fran has recently published his first book, *Act Authentically: An Actor's Workout,* that is becoming a part of his income model and stream along with speaking and teaching. I had recommended that he offer his acting classes online while I was in his workshop. After initially raising his eyebrows and saying nothing, the idea took hold and he is now doing this, along with other fellow creatives in a way that allows him to share his message, one that I consider to be profound, with the world.

CHAPTER THREE

Choosing Your Topic

"Broadly speaking, the short words are the best,
and the old words best of all."
~ Winston Churchill

The topic you initially decide to speak about is the starting point for turning your talk into an ongoing income stream. This will be what is known as your "topic of influence." Over time I want you to tighten this up so that your topic of influence is as specific as possible and unique to you. This may seem challenging at the beginning but is well worth your time in the long run.

I was asked to do a webinar presentation years ago on the topic of earning significant income in my business. At the time I had only a few hundred names on my email list. I had written several blog posts about this and thought of my strategy as using what I referred to as "relationship marketing" to connect with people.

Over time this grew to ten blog posts and that's when I created an outline of the ten things anyone could do to increase their income with a list of only a few hundred names. Then I added ten more actions to my list and when I got up to twenty different actions, I decided that what I was doing in my business and blogging about was valuable enough to turn into a book. I stretched to come up with five more ideas and began doing webinars about my process.

I did not realize it at that time, during the summer and fall of 2009 I was branding myself in a way that would make me a memorable character in my story. I continued to add ideas to my list and write a blog post for each one and my first book - *Huge Profits with a Tiny List: 50 Ways to Use Relationship*

Marketing to Increase Your Bottom Line - was published during the summer of 2010.

Let's say that your topic is life coaching for women in transition because you believe this to be of importance to those who are seeking assistance with their life's path and journey. Perhaps you have received or are working towards a coaching certification. You may have written down some notes on the information you would like to share.

It is likely you know this topic like you know the back of your hand. Blog about it. Write a short report that highlights the specifics of what people need to know and are interested in finding out more about. Talk about it to everyone you know in your daily life. Turn what you've written and told others about into a presentation you can give in person and online and now you're a public speaker on your topic.

Speaking on a "Hot" Topic

Occasionally you will be asked to speak on a topic that is popular, but one that may not be in an area where you have knowledge and experience. This was the case for me when I was asked to speak, first at my Rotary Club and then at the Rotary District Assembly on the topic of using social media to raise funds for non-profit service organizations.

Not only did I have limited experience with social media at that time, I had zero experience with fundraising of any type. But the more I thought about it the more comfortable I felt presenting on this topic that was considered a "hot" one in 2008. Instead of declining the invitation to speak I graciously accepted the challenge and got to work making this topic my own.

What I mean by this is that I used what the leaders of my Rotary District had assigned me to talk about as a starting point in the outline I created. During the first three slides, where I introduced myself and the topic, I made sure to say that I was new to social media and had yet to be anything more than a volunteer for various fundraising events, but what I lacked in experience would be more than compensated for with my enthusiasm and a sincere desire to be of service to others.

Those first three slides made my audience of about three hundred people from all over the world sit up and take notice. They appreciated my transparency and it was immediately noticeable by their facial expressions and body language.

I then proceeded to give them everything I had in terms of the basics of social media, other non-profits using these new platforms strategically, and my thoughts and ideas for using social media to increase our efforts with raising funds. Then I forwarded to a slide that had an image I took from the Rotary International website and a big red question mark I took from Google. The text on my slide said "Your Ideas" and I stepped forward a few steps closer to the audience and said,

"Now it is your turn. I want us to brainstorm ideas together. I've shared my best ones. Many of you have been in Rotary for many years and your experience is a valuable resource we can all benefit from today. Please share your thoughts and ideas now."

It was quiet for just a moment and then hands went up, people began to talk to others sitting at their tables, and people in the back of the auditorium stood up and moved in closer. There was an easel and markers positioned next to where I was standing and someone brought it over even closer to me to facilitate my training.

The next twenty minutes flew by and my hand was tired from writing so much. Everyone was participating and finally the leader of the event came over, took my hand and the microphone, and told the group we had to move on. They gave me a standing ovation and I learned more about public speaking on that day that I could have from reading a dozen books. The point I'm making here is that you must be authentic and true to who you are. And have faith that you will be able to come up with the ideas you need to turn any speaking assignment into a magical experience for everyone in the room.

Take the time to experiment with two or three topics to decide which will be the best "topic of influence" for the goals you are working to achieve with your speaking business. Early on I spoke about real estate because I had worked in that field for twenty years, but it didn't feel right for me.

Speaking About What You Want to Be Known for in Your Speaking Business

At some point in your speaking experience, you will make the conscious decision to speak on the topic you most want to be known for in order to solidify your position. I've done this successfully at two different times. The first time was when I presented the Keynote at a marketing event and chose to talk about my life experiences in a talk I titled "Are You Willing to Do What it Takes?"

During this presentation I shared things about myself that few people outside of my family and close friends were aware of. I had grown up in poverty, raised by my mother in Los Angeles after my parents divorced when I was three years old. At one point I showed a slide with a picture of a laundromat and told the story of how my mother and I had become homeless when I was about eight years old and we slept on the floor of a laundromat on a bed she made from blankets and clothes for a few nights.

On one of those nights I was awoken by the sounds of men out on the sidewalk and suddenly one of them pushed his way into the laundromat. My mother jumped up off the floor and walked quickly to where he was. In a loud, guttural voice I had never heard before come out of her she scolded "Get out of here!" to the one who had come inside. The men had most likely just left a bar down the street when it closed and may have been looking for a bathroom. Her fast thinking and actions had saved us from a situation that could have turned out much differently.

There were audible sobs from the audience members as I continued to share my life, in relation to my topic of being willing to do whatever it takes to achieve success in life and business. I knew this presentation and topic was a powerful one and two years later I wrote and published a book on this topic entitled *Doing What It Takes: An Online Entrepreneur's Playbook.* This one continues to be one of my most popular titles and the one people contact me about to share their feedback and to ask me more questions about the direction their lives are taking.

The second time I spoke on a topic I wanted to be known for was in 2012 at an event in Las Vegas. My objective this time was to introduce myself as a bestselling author and publisher. By that time, I had at least ten titles to my name and I brought a paperback copy of each one up to the stage with me. I placed the stack of books on a small table on the side where a bottle of water had been placed for me.

As I gained momentum, I picked up different titles and shared how I had come to write that particular book. I could feel how powerful my presentation was while I was delivering it. Using a physical item instead of showing images of my book covers on slides made all the difference.

Niche It Down

You will want to go an inch wide and a mile deep with your topic. By this I mean that instead of attempting to attract everyone who has even a slight interest in your overall topic, you will hone in on a smaller group of people who have a specific interest in what you are specializing in with your speaking. This makes sense when you think about it.

As an example, I began my online business by helping people who wanted to write and publish an eBook. For almost two years I explored every nook and cranny around this topic. It was only after I had made a name for myself in this niche that I ventured out into the larger space of online marketing. Even then, I chose to specialize in the areas of information products, affiliate marketing, authorship, and relationship marketing instead of attempting to tackle every niche that was a part of the online marketing space.

I often share the story of someone who spoke regularly about facilitating masterminds. Once when I was on a call with my Mastermind group, none of us could recall her name. I went to Google and typed in "how to create and run a mastermind" and Karyn Greenstreet's name and website came up on page one. I just did that search again and she is still there after all these years. Instead of being just another business coach Karyn chose to specialize in a very specific niche area as her topic of influence.

The ideal scenario is to focus on a smaller niche within your overall topic and to build your business around it, as I did when I took on the topic of how to make huge profits with a tiny list. I still maintain my website for this topic, my book around this topic still sells, and the talk I initially gave has blossomed into a keynote speech and an online course. Being willing to niche down by focusing on a smaller, but well-defined segment of your market makes sense on many levels.

Speaking About the Topic of Your Book

Once you become a published author you will want to create a speech that is directly related to the topic of your book. As you can see, I've done this in reverse on two different occasions. But I have also used this strategy by writing the book first and then creating a presentation around it.

One that I'd like to share with you is from my book *Write. Publish. Prosper. How to Write Prolifically, Publish Globally, and Prosper Eternally.* This is perhaps the most intentional book I have written to date, in that I could see the process of going from idea to book to online course to speech unfolding in my mind as I created the initial outline for the book months before I began writing and creating.

While I was still writing this book, I created an online course to coincide with the chapters and sections of the book. For those who signed up for the course I promised to send them a signed copy of the book when it had published and was available in paperback a few weeks later and after the online course had begun. If you ever need motivation to complete a manuscript, this method works quite effectively! This also gave me the time to get feedback from the more than fifty students who signed up to learn about my "write, publish, prosper" philosophy.

Once the book was published and the first version of the online course had been completed, I then taught the online course live for a second time, at an increased investment to new students, and also began speaking live and online on this topic.

I have also created speeches related to the topics of two of my books, entitled *The Transformational Entrepreneur: Creating a Life of Dedication and Service* and *Rethinking the Work Ethic: Embrace the Struggle and Exceed Your Own Potential.*

I'll share more about how to create your speech based on one of your books in Chapter Five on *Preparing Your Speech*.

Procuring Speaking Engagements

Even though the strategy of how to find the right speaking engagements for what you wish to achieve will be covered in greater detail later on in this book, I thought it important to touch on it here. Procuring speaking engagements that will allow you to move closer to the goal of creating an income based on your speaking is a worthwhile pursuit. I got my start by speaking at Rotary, as I mentioned earlier in this chapter. Rotary is an international service organization and one that does not have political or religious connections. They first asked me to speak when social media was just taking off and I had mentioned that I was learning more about this in order to grow my new online business.

As a writer, I know that the secret to becoming a published author is to write. The same holds true for speakers; you become a speaker by talking about your topic to people who are interested in what you are saying. The key is to get your message in front of the right people. This is what I recommend...

Start out by making it known to the people within your "circles of influence" that you would like to speak about your topic. If you are not familiar with the term "circle of influence" it refers to people with whom you have something in common; you may work in the same physical location or industry, belong to the same church, live in the same neighborhood, or your children may be on the same softball team. Before I started my business online my circles of influence included the teachers at the schools I had worked at, the local real estate board, a tennis club I frequented, and the church I was attending. It would be years later before I understood the power of those groups of people in regards to achieving my goals and dreams.

Every city of significant size – this varies in different locations, but a population of about 50,000 is a good rule of thumb – will have an active Chamber of Commerce and an online calendar of events. Become accustomed to connecting with the people and websites where everyone and everything is listed at least once a week. There are many groups who actively seek out speakers on a regular basis and they will be thrilled when you reach out to them personally.

It is best if you visit each group first, either in person or virtually, to learn more about them and their mission in the community. For example, I was interested in speaking at a quarterly conference hosted by the Boys & Girls Club and decided to attend one of their fundraisers to learn more about them. That evening I met several people who had been active with this group for many years. I introduced myself as a former classroom teacher, foster parent, and Big Sister, as well as an author and speaker. It was one of these people who suggested I apply for a speaking slot at their upcoming conference and I wholeheartedly agreed.

It is my hope that you are excited about the possibilities of speaking on your topic at events of many types. For now, I simply want you to give some thought to the idea that you are responsible for procuring the speaking engagements you want, particularly at the beginning of your public speaking journey. Both Ellen and I will discuss this more fully throughout this book.

CHAPTER FOUR

Defining Your Goals

"What I know for sure is that speaking your truth is the most powerful tool we all have."
~ Oprah Winfrey

Because you are reading this book, Ellen and I will assume that you are already interested not only in a career as a public speaker but that you are also someone who would like to earn a living with your speaking. That is the focus of what we are sharing with you here when we are explaining how to turn your talk into an ongoing income stream. Let's take this one step further and discuss the goal you have as a public speaker on your way to turning it into an income stream.

Earlier I shared that the secret to becoming a published author is to write. This applies to speakers as well; you become a speaker by talking about your topic to people who are interested in what you are saying. The key is to get your message in front of the right people so that you build a following and a platform. The following is what I recommend, in a step-by-step process in order for you to work towards your goals.

First, think about the speakers who have inspired you with their message from the stage. What was it about the person or the message that stuck with you and had you thinking differently almost immediately?

Next, decide what you want to occur after you give your speech. Will people be running to the back of the room and purchasing your product or course? Perhaps they will use their smart phone or tablet to join your list on the spot.

Finally, how will your audience members feel after you speak? Will they describe the experience as enlightening, educational, eye-opening, inspiring, or something else altogether?

To be persuasive in a way that allows you to direct the consciousness of those who hear you speak requires practice. Knowing what you are going for is the ideal way to begin.

Besides wanting to create an income stream based on your speaking, what other goals do you have? This is indeed something to give great thought to, as it is completely up to you and there is no limit to what you will be able to achieve, and quickly in most cases.

Speaking Models

There are so many types of speaking assignments and models you may choose from. Let's begin with these:

- Speaking for pay
- Speaking for a small fee (typically $500 or less)
- Speaking for free, and offer a freebie (corporate, educational, telesummits)
- Speaking for free and also selling, from the stage or in the back of the room

Personally, I have never been paid to speak but my co-author, Ellen Finkelstein has spoken for pay many times throughout her speaking career. As you transition from free to paid, be willing to take a modest fee. Speakers speak. Whatever stage you are at in your paid speaking career, set your fee so you can get hired at least two to three times a month. Throughout my teaching career we had speakers come to the school to present on their topic. Now I know these people were willing to speak to groups of children in order to share their message and have more time honing their talk. This profession takes a lot of practice in front of live audiences. There is no substitute!

One of my clients speaks for small fees in her local community. She ends her presentation by asking attendees to fill out a form if they would like to receive her newsletter and have a complimentary 30-minute phone consultation to talk about their goals. This has been extremely effective and results in new coaching clients for her business every single time.

You also have the choice of speaking in person or virtually. There is online speaking on teleseminars, webinars, virtual summits and more. In person you may be asked to emcee an event, teach on a specific topic, or to deliver a keynote. Or, you may be one of several speakers over a single day or for several days. Let's discuss the pros and cons of each.

In person pros include:

- More connection with attendees and other speakers
- You'll probably convert better by being in front of your audience

Offline cons:

- You have to travel
- It's more expensive
- You'll probably speak to fewer people

Online pros:

- You don't have to travel
- You can speak to unlimited people
- You can speak more frequently

Online cons:

- You have to deal with more technology (webinar software, setup, recording, storage)
- You don't connect as closely with your audience
- Audience members may be distracted as they attempt to multitask during your presentation
- Your conversion may be lower

Another model related to public speaking is to host your own live or virtual events, as well as hosting small group Retreats. I have done this more than seventy times since 2009. So, let's sort these out. There are paid speakers who do not promote anything when they speak and those who sell from the stage, and still others who engage in a hybrid version of these models. You may speak online or in person. And you may be speaking on someone else's stage, virtual or in person, or on your own stage at an event you host or co-host. Your role may be as an emcee, host, speaker, warm up person, or keynote speaker. The event you speak at may run for an hour, typically online, or for several days, online or at a live, in person event.

How do you choose? In the beginning you will take one or both of two paths. The first is to wait until people come to you and ask you to speak on a specific topic. Even though I had spoken at several large marketing events before my first book was published, as soon as I became an author my bookings increased significantly.

The second path is to be proactive and let others know that you are available to speak. You may wish to share a video or audio recording of your presentation, and to write about who you are and what you speak about. Include this information on your website on a page devoted exclusively to educating visitors about your speaking. Also, create what is known as a "speaker one sheet" and make that available as a download on your site. An added note here – make sure your photos are recent ones so people will have no problem recognizing you when you show up in person or on their computer screen!

Expert Status Through Speaking

Putting together a well organized and polished presentation and speaking on your topic is the fast track to expert status. As you continue to do this over time you will discover that your ideas and thought processes will begin to gel together in a new way. You will be able to formulate ideas and opinions that become unique to you. This is what people will pay you for!

One reason I continue to accept speaking engagements for service organizations and groups where my target audience typically does not spend time is so I will have the benefit of hearing questions and comments from a very different perspective than my own. I learned this early on when I shared my first book with my Rotary Club. When I spoke about making huge profits with a tiny list one man raised his hand to ask "list of what?" and I was able to compare it to the database he had for his prospects and clients. I was using jargon that was familiar to my online followers but not to a broader audience.

I am now fortunate enough to be considered an expert in several areas, including local business marketing, online marketing, authorship, and visibility in your niche. My goal is to continuing learning as much as possible in these areas and to then write and speak about them in new and innovative ways.

Anyone Can Become a Public Speaker

Leading up to and throughout the 18th and 19th century, women were banned to speak publicly and were always represented by men in courtrooms, the legislature, and within the religious community as a whole. It was also considered improper for women to be heard in a public setting. An exception to this custom was the Quaker religion that allowed women to speak publicly in meetings of the church, but only on what they deemed to be "necessary for the good of all members."

In the United States, Frances Wright became one of the first female public speakers. She advocated for equal education for women and men through large audiences and through the press. A Black woman named Maria Stewart, also said to be the second female speaker of the United States, lectured in Boston in front of both men and women just four years after Wright in

1832 and 1833 on educational opportunities and abolition for young girls.

Two sisters named Angelina and Sarah Grimké created a platform for public lectures to women. They were the first female agents of the American Anti-Slavery Society. Both sisters traveled across the United States during the years 1837 and 1839, which was only five years after Maria Stewart. The two sisters faced disagreement by churches that did not agree with their public speaking because they were women. Both sisters spoke about how slavery relates to women's rights and why women need equality.

You may not be familiar with the names of these four women, but their courage and persistence opened doors for women that made a difference for everyone as time went on.

As you can see, anyone can become a speaker, no matter where you are right now, your background and previous life experiences, or any of a number of other criteria. In particular, women have literally been able to find their voice with speaking during the past century, unlike in earlier times in our civilization's history. Define your goals and move forward with enthusiasm and determination.

What is Your "Why" for Becoming a Speaker?

I believe it's important to have some discussion around the topic of what your "why" is for starting your business and whether or not this is important as you move forward. In my thinking we must know why we are doing something if our efforts are going to be successful.

During my twenty years as a classroom teacher, I learned how this works firsthand. In the early years I would jump right in with the "what" and the "how to" of what I was teaching. But around my fourth year I began each lesson by explaining why it was important for them to know, understand, and implement the knowledge they were receiving. Overnight the impetus shifted and the students took ownership of their learning. Their "why" became so much more than simply about completing homework assignments and passing tests.

You will want to define your own goals as you pursue a career as a speaker, and then turn your speaking into a viable income stream. The best way to set any goal is by writing it down and reviewing it on a regular basis. I recommend using a planner or journal you can keep on your desk and referring to it every time you have an idea related to your speaking and when you begin to have speaking engagements. It has long been proven that writing down your ideas and goals is exponentially more effective than simply thinking about them from time to time. Become a person who invests in your future by thinking, writing, taking action, and sharing your results.

This is an example of what you might include in your journal or planner:

- Why do you wish to become a public speaker?
- On which topics would you prefer to speak?
- Who will introduce you to the audience? What will they say about you?
- When you visualize yourself speaking to others, where are you and what are you talking about? Be as detailed as possible with this step. Are you with a small number of people in an intimate setting or are you up on stage in front of hundreds of audience members who are eager to hear you speak? Or, are you in your home office and presenting on a webinar that will broadcast around the world?

- While you are delivering your speech, how will the audience react to your ideas? How will they feel? What emotions are they likely to display?
- Will you send those you are speaking to over to your website to download a free gift, while you are speaking or as you are finishing your talk?
- What will you sell during or immediately after you conclude your talk?
- How will you be able to follow up with the attendees, other speakers, and event organizers after it is over?
- What's next? How will you leverage the momentum of your last speaking event to catapult you into speaking at more virtual and live events in the near future?

Over time you will understand the value of these exercises and begin to refer back to what you were thinking earlier. Defining your goals as a speaker and then documenting each step will pay off handsomely in the long run.

Make a Study of Speakers You Admire

Oprah Winfrey was a guest presenter on an awards show I watched on television recently. I observed how she walked out on to the stage after she was introduced and came to a stop right on her mark. I have no idea if she was able to practice this beforehand but it looked to me as though she floated all the way to the podium. Then she clasped her hands in front of her as though she was royalty. The effect was very ethereal and literally set the stage for her to begin.

She began to speak and after a minute or two she unclasped her hands and lifted her arms slowly until they were outstretched. With her palms facing the ceiling Oprah exclaimed "Hallelujah!" by emphasizing every one of the four syllables deliberately, and almost giving the word a musical tone. This brought a standing ovation before she continued.

While I was watching I stood up next to where I was sitting to emulate her movements, and even paused the recording to raise my arms and say "Hallelujah" in a way that worked for me. This was a simple gesture that made her presentation even more memorable at that event.

Richard Branson is not an eloquent speaker, but he does have a presence that is unmistakable. He makes excellent eye contact with those seated in the first couple of rows and uses his entire body to gesture and to get his points across. He also raises his arms and uses his hands as though he is painting a picture and this alone can make your speaking more impactful.

I recommend that you practice telling a story or sharing an experience in front of two or three friends or colleagues to practice your stage presence and see what that feels like. The time and effort you put into this will pay off handsomely when you speak in front of an audience composed of your target market.

Speaking as a Part of Your Job or Career

I would surmise that the majority of people who go into a job or career of any type do not expect to be thrust into the world of public speaking, unless they are a teacher, attorney, or actor. I was a classroom teacher for twenty years and never thought of myself as a speaker of any kind, yet I spoke in front of an audience of children every day and of adults on occasion. There are many jobs and careers that offer this opportunity and the manner in which it is handled can change the trajectory of one's life.

Someone who comes to mind as I am writing this is Dr. Anthony Fauci, who has served as the director of the National

Institute of Allergy and Infectious Diseases (NIAID) since 1984. Who would have thought that he would have so much impact on the world through his speaking when he began his career in medicine so long ago? Certainly not him, I am sure. Yet he has been thrust into the public spotlight at many times throughout his career. This occurred soon after he became the director, when he stepped up to oversee the United States government's medical response to the HIV/AIDS crisis. Thirty years later he has become "America's doctor" and the voice of science and reason with the COVID-19 pandemic. Every word he utters is carefully analyzed and scrutinized as the country moves forward based on the scientific and public health recommendations that he is sharing.

Another of my favorite speakers was the late Ruth Bader Ginsburg, Associate Justice of the Supreme Court of the United States from 1993 until her passing on September 18, 2020. Although public speaking is not the primary focus of someone in Ginsburg's position, she became an icon and a highly sought-after speaker across many areas of interest. Each time I heard her speak I felt like I was a part of history in the making and I always learned something that would help shape my thoughts and beliefs for the future. As a lifelong advocate for human rights and gender equality her spoken words defined the dreams of generations.

The third example I will share here of someone who is expected to speak as a part of their career is Tyler Perry. At the first ever virtual Emmy Awards he was presented with the Governors' Award by the Television Academy. This prestigious award — which was left out of last year's (2019) Emmy's — is given to "an individual, company, organization or project for outstanding achievement in the arts and sciences or management of television which is either of a cumulative nature or so extraordinary and universal in nature as to go beyond the scope of the Emmy Awards presented in the categories and areas of the competition."

Perry shared a story of his grandmother and a quilt she had made for him when he was nineteen. I won't spoil it by sharing the details here but I do encourage you to watch this on YouTube at https://www.youtube.com/watch?v=nTgfVDL1xAo. In less than four minutes he tells a story that lets you know everything you need to know about him personally as a fellow human and professionally as a director and producer.

CHAPTER FIVE

Preparing Your Speech

"Give me six hours to chop down a tree and I will spend the first five sharpening the axe."
~ Abraham Lincoln

Preparation is the key to great success with your speaking. It will also make a difference in the way you are able to turn your speaking into an ongoing revenue stream, which is the main focus of this book. When you are better prepared your speech will be smooth, polished, and professional. It will also be more effective as you work towards your goals.

Before I begin to put together a talk of any type I ask myself three questions. The first is "What is my big idea I want to share with this audience?" In my mind I imagine that the information I will deliver will be life changing, at least for some members of the audience.

The second question is "How will my speech motivate the audience members to take action right away?" When people take quick action on the information I'm sharing, it is the very best gift I can receive.

Finally, I ask myself "What do I want my audience to do next, immediately after I finish speaking?"

Once I outline the answers to these three questions, I get to work on the task of preparing my speech.

For the first question, regarding my "Big Idea" I begin with what I refer to as a "Power Precept." Mine is that I believe anyone can become an entrepreneur if they are willing to learn, implement, and do the work. Think about the big idea you have come up with that can be your power precept. For example, I mentor someone whose power precept is that you can "disappear" depression by changing the way you eat. She did it for herself almost a decade ago and knows it works. Someone else in my inner circle had a big idea about using her voice to reach a massive, global audience and turned that into a precept around podcasting to share your message. Take the time to explore your big idea so you may turn it into your "Power Precept."

The answer to my second question on how I will motivate people to take action comes with time and experience. Sometimes you'll think that your speech fell flat in this area because you didn't hear back from anyone. Then one day, out of the blue someone will contact you and share how your talk motivated them to achieve a goal or change their life in some way. This is quite gratifying and it will happen for you in time.

The third question on what action you would like for your audience members to take immediately is related to what you will ask of them from the stage. Perhaps you want them to join your list or purchase a product. You may also ask them to share something on social media using a specific hashtag or to leave a comment on one of your articles or blog post. Asking people to take a clear and specific action will empower them to interact with you and follow through with what you are sharing with them.

Introducing: The "Signature" Speech

I have shared how I began speaking to grow my business by talking about how I was earning money with my small list of subscribers. Becoming the "huge profits with a tiny list" person, I was able to make a name for myself in the online marketing space. Those who heard me share specific details of how this was working for me hung on to every word and took copious notes. This topic and my presentation became my "signature" speech before I had ever heard or become familiar with that phrase. Ellen goes into great detail on this topic of writing and delivering your signature speech in the following chapter.

Let's define a "signature" speech as one in which you, as the expert and authority are willing and able to answer questions on your topic, expand the depth of your knowledge to include future, hypothetical scenarios, and can impart your knowledge to others. Whether you are delivering your information and ideas virtually or in person, you are the one people think of when they want to know more in this specific area. One of my colleagues, Karyn Greenstreet is known for facilitating masterminds and she writes and speaks on this topic frequently. I mentioned her earlier as an example of speaking for success and an ongoing income stream.

Perhaps this sounds like attempting to fill shoes that are much too large for you right now, but stick with me here and I will explain how creating a signature speech will flow naturally as you move forward with the information you wish to share.

Each of us is an individual, with a lifetime of experiences that cannot be duplicated by anyone else in the world. Others will benefit from learning from our experiences. The way we handled a difficult or challenging situation can become a resource manual to someone who is facing a similar situation. I will share two examples from my personal life.

I was first diagnosed with breast cancer at the age of 37. Without any family history of cancer of any kind I was shocked and had to make some decisions very quickly. First, I attended a support group at the hospital where I was to undergo a radical mastectomy just days later. My assumption when I entered the room was that I would be the youngest woman there, or at least the youngest patient.

I sat down next to a woman in her sixties and introduced myself. After a few minutes of conversation, she looked up and said,

"There's my daughter now. She's beginning chemotherapy in the morning and I wanted her to come tonight."

My assumption turned out to be completely unfounded when I was introduced to this young woman. She had just turned twenty-four and was fighting Stage 3 breast cancer.

Over the next fourteen months I underwent three surgeries and multiple types of medical treatments that ultimately saved my life. This became my personal story and one that was unique to me. When I reached the three-year mark, I was invited to become a volunteer with the American Cancer Society. Each woman I met with had their own situation and I shared my story with them. What I shared with them was my "signature" story of what I had experienced, what I had learned, and how they could benefit from what I had gone through to better prepare for their own cancer journey.

The next time I created a "signature" talk was when I decided to become a real estate appraiser. This began when I was in the office where I had been working as a real estate agent and an appraiser stopped by to review some of our public files. After a brief conversation with him I asked him how I could get into this highly sought after and lucrative field. He told me it would be next to impossible for me to break in, especially because I was a woman. I thanked him for his time and returned to my desk. Of course, I now wanted to become a real estate appraiser more than anything.

Six months later I was doing just that and my story became both inspiring and helpful to others as they decided to break into this field as well. Over the next decade I told my story dozens of times to real estate groups and to people looking for a new career. They all benefitted from hearing about my situation and what I did to make it work out positively for myself. Many people thanked me for helping them go in this direction and for pointing out the mistakes and pitfalls to avoid.

We all feel like we do not have anything special or unique to share with others when we are getting started, but that simply isn't true. Take some time to think about what you have to offer other people. Make some notes that include your thoughts, ideas, and experiences. Choose one area and flesh it out as an outline of what you could talk about. Typically, we all take for granted the knowledge we already have and do not realize the positive impact it will have on even one other person.

Years ago, I was at a meeting for people interested in technology and using computers. This was during the late 1980s when technology was in its infancy for the general public. Some of us were standing together and someone asked me about investing in real estate. I do not remember exactly what I said that night, but I did talk about how to buy one single family home and rent it out to get started as an investor. Then I explained how to purchase a second property as soon as possible to begin creating some passive income.

The following month a lady named Dorothy came up to me before the meeting began and told me she had given notice to her employer and was relocating to a beach community a few hours north of where she was living at that time. She told me that what I had said the previous month had inspired her to start living the life she wanted right now, instead of waiting for something that might not ever happen.

As she thanked me, I searched for the right words to say and to recall exactly what I had said to the group. This could have become my signature story and talk if I had taken the time to deconstruct the ideas I had spoken of and outlined. In fact, I had learned much of what I was doing by reading the books and listening to presentations from real estate investor Robert Allen. His book *Nothing Down: How to Buy Real Estate for Little or No Money Down* got me started when it was published in January of 1984. Allen turned this topic into his signature speech and topic and continues to share his knowledge and experiences with others throughout the United States and Canada.

Your words are powerful and can move mountains when you talk to others. What have you accomplished in your life that took time and effort and perseverance? Begin with the obvious, like finishing college, starting a family, or entering a new career. Move on to the challenges and difficulties you encountered. How did you deal with setbacks? What strategies did you explore? Why were you able to succeed where others had failed or given up? The answers to these questions will guide you as you create a speech that will move others to action and help change their lives.

Creating Your Outline

Now it's time to create an outline for your speech. An outline is a road map that takes you and your audience member from where you/they are right now to closer to where you want for them to be. Just as we must plan and organize a trip we take in a car, on a plane, or with any other mode of transportation, so must we plan and organize our speech. I do this each morning before I go for my one hour walk and I did it when I took my cross-country road trip a few summers ago. Once I understood the value of outlining, I began creating outlines for my writing as well as for my speeches and presentations.

Begin by reviewing your answers to the three questions I posed at the beginning of this chapter. Write down your "Big Idea" and the "Power Precept" behind it. Use this to come up with a title that will grab the interest of those who may be in your audience. This also arouses curiosity around you and your topic.

Next, share some information about yourself. Perhaps most of your audience is already familiar with you, but if even one person is not you do not want to omit this step.

I like to talk about where I was before I came online. Working as a classroom teacher and also running my own real estate business from home gives me a unique perspective on business, I believe. After coming online my time was my own and I began writing and creating information products.

After a few years I had replaced, and then surpassed my previous income and had also become a published author. I was then able to travel the world, host my own live events and retreats, and have a greater impact on the world. I did this through the charities and non-profits I had aligned myself with and I had begun volunteering with them both locally and in countries around the world.

This is the "before, after, after" strategy that works so well.

Before I was working as a teacher and simultaneously as a real estate broker and residential appraiser. I was exhausted from working long hours and had little savings to show for it.

After coming online, I learned how to replace my previous income and have more time to myself.

After I'd been working as an online entrepreneur for about eighteen months, I surpassed my previous income and decreased my working hours down to fewer than twenty each week.

Then I answer the four questions, a strategy I learned from working with thought leader and marketer Alex Mandossian early on. This was part of my quest for entrepreneurial success at that time. I was just beginning to speak publicly and needed direction as to how to create speeches and presentations that would be meaningful and impactful to my audiences. Alex had adapted the questions from teachings by Simon Sinek, author of the bestselling *Start with Why: How Great Leaders Inspire Everyone to Take Action*. The questions are as follows:

- WHY is [TOPIC] so important for our audience to learn more about?
- WHAT is [TOPIC] by definition?
- HOW does [TOPIC] work in a step-by-step process?
- WHAT IF our listeners utilized the strategies you are teaching us about [TOPIC], what would their lives be like in 30 days, 90 days, 1 year?

Let's take a closer look at each of these questions and how you may use them to create an outline for your speech. By starting with "Why?" in regard to your topic of influence you are choosing to speak about, you have the opportunity to grab your audience's attention immediately. I think of this as the title of my talk and the headline I would use to share it with others. This allows you to teach and explain your topic, knowing that you have captured their interest along with that attention.

But even though we start with the why of how our topic is of great importance I continue to start teaching during my speeches and presentations by defining what my topic is in language that will be clear and understandable to everyone in the audience. I learned long ago that people may not understand exactly what you are referring to with your topic and you don't want to lose them right away or they will be gone forever.

I discovered this when I shared a copy of my brand-new book with my Rotary Club back in 2010. The title is *Huge Profits with a Tiny List: 50 Ways to Use Relationship Marketing to Increase your Bottom Line*. Tony, a member who owned an automobile dealership raised his hand and asked "A list of *what*?" in reference to my title. I quickly answered that it was similar to the database of clients and prospects for his business and then he understood.

Then I move on briefly to the third question on how it all works. I will come back to this question and answer it in great detail throughout my talk. But first I will move on to the fourth question about what my audience can expect if they are willing to follow through with my strategies and methods. Let's take a closer look at the pieces of a well-prepared presentation:

- Introduce yourself and the name of your talk. Ellen refers to this as your "Authority Story" and you'll want to practice this part to make sure it comes across as you wish and does you justice.
- Introduce your "Power Precept."
- Share an agenda of what you will be sharing with them that day.
- Introduce yourself in greater detail, using the "before, after, after" method I discussed above. This also lets your audience members know why you are qualified to talk to them on your topic.
- Tell them why your topic is important for them. Share two perspectives so they have more details to connect with in terms of how your topic will be valuable for them.
- Return to the "why" and present more details emphasizing the importance of your topic.
- Give them one strategy, explaining how they can achieve results around your topic that will benefit them personally.
- Discuss the "what if" so they will be able to visualize what is possible for them if they are willing to focus on you and what you are sharing.

- Return to the "how" and include as much detail as possible during the remainder of the time you have with them.
- Give them a recap of what you have just shared with them. This is similar to the three-part essay we learned to write in school; you tell them what you're going to tell them, tell them, then tell them what you have just told them. This works every time.
- Briefly remind them of what you have been able to achieve and then make the offer you have decided to share at the end of your presentation.

Throughout your talk you will want to ask your audience if the information is helpful and allude to the product or program you will be selling or giving away at the end. This is the concept of "micro-commitments" where your audience members nod in agreement along the way and are anxious to consume what you have to offer long before you have asked them to take that next step of taking advantage of your offer.

I now think of my presentations as ones in which I inform and educate my audience, as well as entertaining them throughout the time I am on stage, physically or virtually. But I was much too nervous and inexperienced to accomplish this when I first began speaking. I simply created my outline as I have described it here and delivered my information with precision and integrity.

Also, you'll want to create two versions of your speech. One will be a talk you can deliver in 45 minutes to an hour. The other will be a shortened version that can be delivered in 20 to 30 minutes. This will cover everything, from TED talks to keynotes to speeches you will deliver at service clubs like Rotary. In each case you will take a few questions at the end. Your host may also wish to ask you some questions at the end that were not covered in sufficient detail during your presentation or are of personal interest to them. Be prepared to field all types of questions. Some may seem off target, but you will be able to answer in a way that makes sense.

It's important for the audience members to see themselves in you while you are speaking. This will allow them to live vicariously through your experiences and imagines themselves living a version of this life within the structure of the life they have created for themselves.

This is particularly important when you are selling from the stage, as the products, courses, and programs you offer will be an extension of your talk, and of you. When they can imagine taking you home with them in their briefcase, placing you on the bookshelf next to their computer, taking you outside and sharing a cup of coffee with them on their patio, and having conversations with you whenever they want, you've earned the sale before you have even made your offer.

While remembering that each one of us is a unique individual, focus on the many things we all have in common. These may include:

- having loved ones we want to provide for
- having the desire to help others in need
- seeing the value in empowering those who need a hand up
- wanting to leave a legacy for the future

The things that unite us are always much greater than those that divide us. Think of speaking as a way to connect with others and to be open to their unique perspectives on topics we may believe have only one side and solution. You will become the ultimate communicator as a public speaker.

Creating a Speech Based on Your Book

As I mentioned earlier, I have put together speeches and presentations based on my books numerous times. In a way, your book is the perfect outline for your speech. The premise is the central theme. The "big idea." The details within your speech prove your premise and precept in no uncertain terms.

For each precept, you may want to give an explanation, then an example, and finally the action steps for this audience. Or, for each concept, you have an option to use the timeline formula: Past, Present, Future. It may also serve your message to use the success formula of stating the problem, exploring a solution, and sharing some examples. Be sure to tell the stories you will share through the eyes of two characters, to prove your concepts are universal.

Share a great story for every point. Read through your book and make note of which you consider to be the best stories. Use those stories in your speech.

In order to market your book where you are speaking, give copies away as a prize. Ask for a volunteer and ask questions and give each person your book as a prize. People will want to answer your questions and volunteer to help you, and the others will want to purchase your book.

Preparation Includes Lots of Practice

Preparing your speech is important and practicing what you have created will ensure that you have included everything you want to share. Practice will also add to your level of confidence and allow for a smoother delivery of your content. I have been known to practice my speeches and presentations 100 times before going in front of an audience.

As I am preparing my presentation, I will stand up in my home office and deliver it out loud to myself in the full-length mirror on my door. At this point I can see and feel right away if something needs to be reworded or explained more clearly.

Before going too far into this, get some feedback from friends and colleagues. Ask them to be honest and constructive in their comments to you. Do they feel your information is valuable? Is it interesting and compelling? What do they not understand or feel is stated in a way that turns them off or alienates them?

Now it's time to write out every word of your speech. As you speak it out, make sure to record and time it. You almost always have a time constraint and won't know if you'll meet it unless you practice and time it. Later I'll be sharing the details of a speech I had to deliver in just under four minutes for something called "Better Your Best" so I wouldn't be disqualified. I won't spoil it now by telling you what happened and how the outcome changed the trajectory of my life.

Watch the recording and make notes, then edit your script. Now listen to it without watching to hear it differently. Make more edits. Practice until it's smooth, but it doesn't have to be perfect. You don't want to be reading when you speak but you still want to stay on topic, share your message with passion and integrity, and finish within your allotted time. Maintain a spirit of excitement and enthusiasm, as this will be powerful.

Now we'll move on to Ellen's chapter on *Writing and Delivering Your Signature Speech.*

CHAPTER SIX

Writing and Delivering Your Signature Speech

"But maybe the most powerful infectious thing is the act of speaking the truth."
~ Vera Nazarian

If every time someone asks you to speak on any topic, you say yes, you won't do yourself or your audience justice.

You have knowledge that can transform lives and that's what you should be speaking about. In this way, you'll become known as an expert on that topic and gain authority in that field.

This focus will bring you more invitations to speak than if you speak on anything and everything. It will also save you lots of time, because creating a new speech each time you speak is lots of work!

Your *signature speech* is the one you do most of the time, on your area of expertise. It's the topic that makes you stand out from all the other speakers who speak on similar topics.

This doesn't mean you can't speak on other, usually related topics. You can even have a portfolio of topics, but you'll usually have one main speech that establishes your reputation and is the foundation of your online business.

Your signature speech is your primary way to transform lives and make an impact.

Another Reason for a Signature Speech

Besides sticking with your expertise and getting more opportunities to speak, there's another reason to have a signature speech and that's all about turning your speaking into a business, a stream of income.

Your signature speech leads to a funnel—a series of offers - that you have developed and that you know works. More accurately, your signature speech is the first step of a funnel. This funnel is repeatable.

Every talk you give should lead to another step in your funnel so that it grows your business. However, your funnel can vary based on the type of speaking you do.

Let's look at some scenarios:

- If you're paid to speak, you usually don't sell anything. But you can always offer a free resource or mention your book (if you have one). The free resource would require an opt-in so that your audience members become your subscribers. You then make offers to your subscribers. Your book should similarly have an offer. For more information on how to do that, see our book, *Authors! The Quick Book to Business Method.* (You can buy it on Amazon at amzn.to/31HCq1B.)
- If you're selling from the stage or at the back of the room, you make your offer right away. For people who don't buy, you can still offer a free resource.
- You might offer a free 1-on-1 consultation so some members of the audience - based on their interest or as a prize - and you can then convert those people to customers.

Decide how your funnel will work BEFORE writing your signature speech.

Decide on Your Goal

The goal of speaking is always for change. You want to help your audience grow and achieve their own goals. You have a solution to their problem and you want to inspire them to implement it.

Of course, you can't create miracles in one hour. But you can give your audience practical steps they can take right away and motivate them to move forward in their life and/or business.

What type of transformation can YOU create when you speak?

Your second goal is to get as many people as possible into your funnel. The point here is that your funnel is what both moves people to achieve their goals using your solution to their problem AND what enables you to earn an income helping others. It's a win-win situation.

Know Your Audience

In order to create the change in your audience, you need to know who they are. If you get this wrong, you won't help them and they won't respond to your message. Knowing your audience is one of the first rules of speaking.

Here are some ways you can find out about your audience:

- Ask the event organizer
- Send them a questionnaire in advance
- Do a poll at the beginning of your talk

Recently, I was hosting a web summit on presentation skills. One of the speakers had assumed that most of the attendees would be presentation designers, which they weren't. In fact, 70% of them were trainers. (We knew this because we had previously done a poll, asking them what type of presentations they did.) Luckily, I caught the problem and we changed her topic to be a better match.

In general, you want to avoid speaking to an audience that isn't in your target market. But each audience is slightly different, of course, so you should be able to incorporate minor changes into your signature speech so that audience members feel like you are talking directly to them.

I often do a poll at the beginning of a talk. Besides the fact that it gives me valuable information about the audience, it engages them right at the beginning and they're more likely to pay attention to the rest of what I want to say.

If you're doing an in-person talk, you can ask people to raise hands. (There are systems that let them answer on their cellphone, if you want to get more exact numbers.)

If you're using a webinar service, use the Poll feature. If you don't have that feature, ask people to use the Chat box.

Give Your Signature Speech an Attention-Getting Title

The name of your signature speech is very important because that is what people use to decide whether to attend. You want your target market to feel that the webinar will solve their most pressing problem. The word "feel" is important here – your title should elicit some emotion while also making clear what you will cover.

Your signature speech can have a main title and a subtitle, just like a book. The subtitle is sometimes called a tag line and lets you elaborate on your topic.

Here are some ideas for naming your signature speech. By the way, these ideas work for sales page headlines, too!

- **Use statistics:** For example, "How to Increase Your Conversion Rate by 50% in the Next 30 Days"
- **Start with a number:** For example, "3 Steps to a Successful Online Business." I have a webinar called, "10 Hacks for Better Slides in Under 5 Minutes" that attracts a lot of attendees. For some reason, 3, 5, 7 and 10 are popular numbers.
- **Make a promise:** For example, "Create Your Online Product in a Weekend"

- **Say that your content is new:** For example, "New Ways to Connect on Social Media" or "Hot Design Techniques that Are Trending Now"
- **Mention your target market:** For example, "3 Ways Life Coaches Like You Can Get More Clients"
- **Mention your target market's problem:** For example, "Stop Procrastinating and Get Your First Product Out the Door Now!"
- **Make It Sound Easy:** For example, "3 Easy Steps to Create Low-Content Products"
- **Mention Their Fear:** For example, "5 Ways to Get More Clients from Social Media Without Spending Hours Each Day" or "How to Get Your First Product Out the Door, even if You Are a Newbie at Technology"

Why don't you brainstorm some titles for your signature speech right now?

Once you do that, you can always ask for some feedback from colleagues. It's always worthwhile to test some titles and see which one gets the best results.

Write Your Outline

Your next step is to write an outline for your signature speech. While you obviously have a lot of latitude in what you'll say, there is a useful structure for a speech. This structure is similar to that of a book, in fact, but it's obviously more condensed. In the previous chapter, Connie gave several possible speech structures that you can also use.

Here's a simplified version of the structure:

1. Focus on your audience (target market)
2. Describe the problem they're facing
3. Outline your solution and why it's unique and effective—this is where you put your main content
4. Inspire them to act

Now, we're going to unpack those four components to give you a big head start in writing your signature speech. You can copy this outline and expand on it with your unique content.

1. Tell them what to expect

People want to immediately know that they'll get value from your talk. They want to know that you'll help them move toward their goals or overcome their obstacles. The title of your talk should make this clear, but you should repeat it when you start.

2. Share your story and credibility

The next thing people want to know is why you can give them that value. Who are you? How did you gain your knowledge, experience or expertise? How many people have you helped?

If you tell this in story form, it will be much more engaging and sound less like an infomercial for yourself. Don't spend too long on this. At the end, people should feel comfortable with who you are and believe that you can help them.

3. Share what you will teach them

Now, explain what you will cover in a little more detail. This can be a list of topics. For example, if you are giving them 3 easy steps to low-content products, you can list the steps here.

Don't go into detail because that's coming up soon.

4. Tell them you'll let them know where they can find out more at the end

This is obviously a reference to your offer. You can specifically say you'll make an offer at the end. I find that to be more honest and the audience appreciates that.

5. Speak out your main content

Here is where you teach and fulfill the promise of your title and webinar sales page. For each point:

1. Name the concept
2. Explain the concept
3. Give an example or metaphor
4. Show how to apply the concept
5. Tell a story of how you or one of your clients used the concept because people want to know that it works
6. Review the concept and make a recommendation for how they can take action on the concept

6. Make your offer

If you'll be making an offer, now is the time to transition to your offer.

Start by summarizing the points you made and emphasize their importance to your audience. Also mention why this knowledge is so important to you – your commitment to helping people.

Ask if they got value from your main points. Getting a "yes" or a description of the "aha" points helps your audience realize that you have given them something of value already.

Compliment them for listening through to the end and mention that this means they're persistent and committed – which is true!

Explain that you have a special offer for them. This could be a product that they can buy right away or a 1-on-1 session to see if they could become a client.

Delve into the offer – its name, benefits, and features.

If you're selling a product, state the regular value and the price for them. Often, these are not the same thing. It's typical to offer a discounted price to your audience. You can use three techniques:

- **Discount:** Offer a discount
- **Bonuses:** Add bonuses
- **Deadline:** Give a deadline for the discount and/or bonuses

Show testimonials or otherwise explain the outcome they will get.

Explain the next steps. Maybe they click a link in the chat. Itemize what they should do after that. For example, if they'll be making an appointment to talk 1-on-1 with you, explain the process.

If you're setting up appointments for a 1-on-1 session, clearly explain what they'll get out of that session.

If you're offering 1-on-1 sessions or a course that starts soon, let them know if there are limitation such as the number of spots available or a time deadline.

Ask for questions about the content of the webinar and your offer. You can have FAQs ready and start by saying, "Many people ask this..." and then answer that question. Continue to answer questions for as long as possible.

As you close, invite them to email you if they have further questions.

If you won't make an offer for a product or a 1-on-1 session, offer something for free or mention your book. This takes a lot less time, but you should still make sure your audience knows the value they'll get from it, the price (if any), and the steps they need to take.

What better time than now to write your outline? (This book will still be here when you come back.)

Expand Your Outline into a Speech

Once you have your outline, expand it into a speech. Then you'll research some statistics and quotes, write out your stories, collect testimonials, and so on. Add those to your speech.

In my experience, it's a mistake to write your speech before you have an outline. I've seen over and over that the result is disorganized and ineffective.

Moreover, the rewriting required makes the whole process take MORE time than it would if you started with an outline. (The same is true for writing a book.)

Another mistake is to start creating slides at this point. Before you've practiced and times your speech, you don't know how many slides you need. You'll almost certainly waste time creating slides that you don't need!

Practice

Practice is necessary for all the talks you give. With your script in hand, speak out your talk, while recording it. I recommend videotaping it, which you can do on Zoom, with your phone, or with your webcam's software.

One of the most important bits of information you'll get from this exercise is how long your signature speech takes. In most cases, you'll want it to take about 45 minutes. That will leave time for questions so that the entire event will last one hour. Sometimes the event organizer will give you a different amount of time, such as 50 minutes for everything, including questions.

It's absolutely essential that you don't go over your allotted time!

Watch the video and take notes of places where you want to make changes. Was something disorganized? Unclear? Poorly worded? Boring? Lacking in emotional impact? Full of "ums" and "you knows?" Did you fiddle with your hair?

Make adjustments both in the content, the timing, and delivery.

The next step is to get feedback from others. Remember, this is your signature speech. It's special and it needs to be top-notch. You can test it with a small audience. If you can record this, too, it really helps to see your body language.

Once your content is finalized, create the slides if you'll use them.

Here are some more practice tips:

- Practice asking and answering questions
- Speak with enthusiasm and energy
- Look directly at your audience; if you're online, look at the webcam
- Stand up when you speak, even in front of your computer – this is a secret of energetic webinars!)

Deliver Your Speech

Before you deliver your speech, make sure that your back-end funnel is all set up and working. Test it! We talk more about the technical aspect of your funnel in Chapter 8.

Be prepared for mishaps. The Internet can fail, PowerPoint can crash, your website can go down, etc. Sometimes, you just have to be graceful in the midst of chaos! But you can have a printout of your script, have an alternative computer available, and so on, just in case.

When you speak, get your energy level up higher than usual. Be aware that everyone is a little nervous but just go out there and do it! You don't have to be perfect but if you've practiced, you'll probably be just fine. Your audience wants you to succeed and is usually fairly forgiving.

"Break a leg," as they say in the theater business...

Follow up

Follow up is essential for any talk. If you're speaking online or offer a freebie, you can automate a lot of the follow up with email autoresponders.

Follow up is the key to turning your signature speech into an online business. Part II of this book explains this process in much more detail.

Don't make the mistake of following up just once. It isn't enough. People are busy and they leave decisions to the last minute. They need to hear from you over and over.

If you're speaking at an event organized by someone else, ask for feedback. Use the feedback, which can be painful, to improve.

Track Results

Because your signature speech has a goal to move audience members into your funnel, you can track its conversion rate. What percent of people signed up? Bought from you? Made an appointment?

Track the conversion rate each time you speak. Here are steps you can take if the conversion is low:

- Be careful to speak only to relevant audiences
- Adjust your speech to be more compelling
- Change your offer to make it more relevant.
- Consider price changes to see which price gets you the best result
- Follow up more after the speech

Part II
Turning Your Speech into a Business

"Great leaders communicate and great communicators lead."
~ Simon Sinek

Part II is about the strategy and technology of turning your speech into a business.

In Chapter 7, I talk about the importance of relationships. This is crucial for speakers because when you speak, you're generally alone in front of your audience, but a business can't exist without others – customers and partners. This chapter also includes an interview with Rebecca Morgan, a highly successful speaker, consultant, and trainer.

Chapter 8, The Art and Science of the Funnel, explains the process of using your speech to make a free offer to get subscribers so that you can sell them products and services. This chapter gets a little technical, but follow along, because you'll need to understand the basics of an online business. I'll also discuss the models of speaking for a fee and selling from the stage – and how they translate into an online business.

Chapter 9 covers the many ways to create relationships via email.

Chapter 10 is about developing your business on your website and creating a selling platform for your products and services. I also cover 4 possible funnels that you'll want to consider.

In Chapter 11, I explain how to use social media to grow your business—and how to use social media strategically without wasting time.

CHAPTER SEVEN

Importance of Relationships

"Trust is the glue of life. It's the most essential ingredient in effective communication. It's the foundational principle that holds all relationships."
~ Stephen Covey

You can't create a thriving business by yourself. You need to build relationships. Of course, you need an audience when you speak. But to turn your speaking into a business, you will need customers and clients—yet they aren't enough.

You might be surprised by that statement, but the truth is that it's almost impossible to get enough customers and clients in your business just by your own efforts. You...

- won't reach enough people
- will have to work too hard to reach enough people
- will spend too much money reaching enough people

For this book, we're focusing on creating relationships with your audience—people who have heard you speak. When you do this properly, audience members become customers.

Without creating a relationship with your customers, you'll struggle because while you might make some sales, the true gold is in repeat sales – and these require a relationship.

As a speaker, your words create a relationship with your reader. Audience members feel like they get to know you through what you say. But to turn your speaking into a thriving business, you need more.

In this chapter, we'll talk about how to create the relationships that turn your speaking into a business.

Relationships Are the Start of Transformation

Your audience wants a transformational experience. They get that by applying what you teach or by the immersive nature of – or the message in -- what you say.

They want to be changed or inspired by what they hear. When you can create a transformational experience, you'll have audience members asking for more! As a result, you have an opportunity to create a relationship with them – to offer them related products or services.

If you write non-fiction, you're more likely to offer related products or services, such as self-study courses and coaching. Ideally, you can then turn one purchase into additional purchases.

And the deeper and closer the relationship, the better the opportunity for a transformation – because one speech might not be enough, right? To really change lives, you need some give and take with people. You need to find out exactly what they need and give it to them. You need to listen to them.

But how do you create relationships without dealing with all of your audience members one-on-one? Doing that would involve so much of your time that you wouldn't be able to help many people at all!

The key is to create a structure of products and services that meet the needs of as many people in your target market, demographic or psychographic as possible. Some products will be low-cost and many people will be able to use them. Others will be more expensive but give people a more customized solution to their needs.

Let's talk more about how you can use the one-way relationship you create in your talk into a more complex relationship that creates a money-making business.

The important thing to remember is when you continue the relationship you:

- Have more opportunities to help people
- Can create a business that starts with your talk
- Can make more money

Relationships are Key to Creating a Money-Making Business from Your Speech

When you speak, you often don't automatically get a way to contact your reader. However, there ARE ways to speak and get immediately access to your audience. One way is to host a webinar. In that case, you get the attendee's name and email address. Later in this book, we'll talk more about creating and maintaining relationships with email.

But if you're speaking in front of a live audience, you need to convince your reader to contact you. The most common way to do this is to have an offer at the end of the talk.

The offer is almost always for something free that is related to your talk. It can be a report, worksheet, video, audio, template, checklist – anything that will help your audience get more value from what you said.

In order to get that free offer (often called a freebie or lead generator), your reader has to fill out a form, providing a name (usually just the first name) and a valid email address. The form could be a paper form if you're in front of a live audience. If it's on your website, the form contains code that you get from your email service provider and it stores the data so that you can subsequently send emails to the reader. More about that later...

Note: Your email service provider also gives you the framework to send out multiple emails in compliance with spam, privacy, and other laws.

Without techniques for creating relationships with your audience, you are likely to lose track of them after they hear you speak. But when you create a relationship, you can discover what they want, make them relevant offers, and grow your business.

Before we delve deeper into this process, let's talk about how you can get that all important name and email address from your audience, whether you're selling from the stage – or at the back of the room – or not.

Techniques for Collecting Information from Your Audience

Speakers have developed many techniques for getting the name and email address of their audience members. Before we start, make sure that it's clear that they'll end up on an email list and get your regular emails, not just whatever freebie you offer them. This is for both legal and ethical reasons.

When Speaking in Front of a Live Audience

Here are some ways to ask for the information when you're speaking in front of a live audience:

- Have a table at the back with a form people can fill out and tell them about it when you speak.
- But a sheet on each chair and invite people to subscribe to get something for free. They can fill out a tear-off, for example
- Ask people to put their business card (or a sheet of paper with the contact info) in a bowl and do a quick raffle for a prize. Make sure they know they'll end up on your list, though.
- Display a slide with the URL of your opt-in page (make it very simple to type) and ask people to go there on their phone to get your free offer. Make the text large and give them time to type it in and fill out the form.

Tip: Leave out https:// and www. If your website's URL is long, use a redirect such as bitly.com and goo.gl. I have a special website just for this purpose, ellenhelps.me and use Pretty Links on that site to create short URLs.

- If there's an organizer with you, ask that person to repeat the URL. Or maybe the organizer can include the link in a follow-up email.
- Ask people to raise their hand if they want your freebie. You can say, "If you would like to get my eBook, please raise your hand." Then tell them to go to their browser on their phone and type in the URL. This method uses social proof, because audience members see that others want the freebie.
- If you created a download just for the talk, tell them it will go away in a few days and they'll probably forget, so they should sign up right away. This uses the principle of scarcity to get people to act.

Tip: You can use texting technology (it's called "text to subscribe" and ask people to text SUMMARY (or anything) to a number on their phone. They'll be asked for their email address and then get an email with the link to your freebie. Search for "text to subscribe." EZTexting is a popular one. Be sure to choose an option that can integrate with your email service.

When Speaking Online

One of the advantages of speaking online is that if you organize the meeting or use your own software, people have to register to attend. You automatically get the information you need. But what if you're speaking as a guest?

Here are some ways to ask for the information when you're speaking online as a guest:

- Put the link to your free offer in the meeting/webinar software's chat box, so people can just click it to go to your opt-in page. You can ask your host to do this for you.

- If you're speaking on a podcast or for a blog post, ask the host to put the link in the podcast notes or blog post text.
- Display a slide with the URL of your opt-in page (make it very simple to type) and ask people to go there on their phone to get your free offer. Make the text large and give them time to type it in and fill out the form.

Tip: As I mentioned earlier for speaking in front of a live audience, leave out https:// and www. If your website's URL is long, use a redirect such as bitly.com and goo.gl. I have a special website just for this purpose, ellenhelps.me and use Pretty Links on that site to create short URLs. Connie's special URL is connieloves.me. Those websites don't contain any content – they are only for creating short, special links.

Opportunities and Techniques for Creating Relationships in an Online Business

So how do you create and develop meaningful relationships with many readers at one time? You develop something called a "funnel." In the next chapter, we'll go deeper into funnels, but for now, you should understand that a funnel draws the reader into a series of emails and then purchases.

Just as a real funnel starts large and has a small opening at the bottom, the number of audience members and potentials audience members may be large but a smaller number flow through to become your subscribers and then customers. However, without a funnel, there is almost no flow-through. You would only hear from the most fanatic readers who go out of their way to find you.

The funnel is the mechanism for you to create a relationship with your readers. You help them to get more out of your talk while helping them to get to know you and what else you have to offer. The funnel is what lies between your talk and a thriving business.

An Interview with Rebecca Morgan

I (Ellen) have known Rebecca Morgan for years as the co-editor of SpeakerNet News, an email newsletter for speakers. But she's also been a speaker for years and is a long-time member of the NSA (National Speakers Association). Finally, she's a consultant and trainer. I interviewed her for this book because I thought she was an excellent example of someone who has turned her speaking into a business.

~ ~ ~ ~ ~

Ellen: Rebecca, what topic do you speak on?

Rebecca: For my corporate audiences, I speak on my 27th book, which was a couple years ago, called *Leadership Lessons from Silicon Valley.*

Ellen: What would you say is your speaker model for your speaking business?

Rebecca: It is a lot of my delivering, keynotes, workshops, retreats or moderating panels. But then I have some products, I have 20 books, and I have some programs where I meet with managers to learn to deliver some of my content to their team on a monthly basis; they get a module each month to deliver.

Ellen: So, you speak for a fee, doing keynotes and workshops. And you get paid to do those. How have you taken that speaking, and then turned it into a business that's more than just getting paid for speaking?

Rebecca: I offer other ancillary services to clients that I'm introduced to via my speaking. I mentioned the monthly program for the managers. Or consulting-- I typically will do a project and there's a goal with the project and the speaking is a way to accomplish that goal. But it often includes other things, like assessments, 360s, consultations, or coaching, depending on what we're trying to accomplish.

Ellen: So you've expanded your speaking business into that monthly program and consulting on the topic of leadership?

Rebecca: My sweet spot is around what Silicon Valley companies have done that make them excel. And there's a concept called psychological safety, which I'm one of the few experts in the world on.

Ellen: How did you get to become an expert on it?

Rebecca: I studied the heck out of everything that I could find about it.

Ellen: You also created a business around speaking, Speaker Net News. Could you describe that?

Rebecca: That's a free weekly ezine for around 9,000 International speakers, trainers and consultants. We also have authors and coaches where we share best practices. You send in your best practice, I cull it down to the nub, then we aggregate those weekly, curate them and send them back out to our mailing list. Plus, we do biweekly webcasts and teleseminars, where I interview people like you, an expert on a specific topic that would be of interest to our readers and we charge for that. We don't charge for the ezine, but we charge for the educational elements.

Ellen: So that's the way you monetize that part of the businesses -- with those webinars that you charge for. Yes, I remember years ago when you interviewed me.

I'd love to know how you got started speaking.

Rebecca: I was a secretary and I attended lots of professional development courses at my institution and the training director finally, after three years of that, or maybe a year and a half of that, said, "Would you teach a class for us?"

And I said, "Well, I'm happy to do so. But what on?"

And she said, "Assertiveness" and I said, "Well, I've never taken a class on assertiveness, but I'm happy to put one together" because she said I live my life really assertively creating win-win situations with the people I've worked with.

So that got the buck in my ear and I did that for a couple years. It grew until I was making more money doing this on the side than I was at my real job so I decided to cut the ties and go independent.

Ellen: Good for you! That's a great story. I have a couple of stories like that where people asked if I could do something and I said yes, even though I didn't know how to do it, because I knew I could do it.

You've written 28 books or so, right? How'd you get into writing books? Let's talk about that.

Rebecca: Years ago, in 1987 or so, I was doing all these seminars in the evenings for bankers where I could sell product at the back of the room. I sold mentors' products, typically. I found this local publisher who lives 20 minutes from my house, and he had created these books called the Crisp books, because that was his last name, but they call them 50-minute books, books that you could read in 50 minutes, and they were interactive.

And so I talked to him about letting me sell some of his titles on commission, actually consignment, at the back room of my seminars, and I sold so many in a short amount of time that he said, "Would you write one of these books for me on selling?"

So, I did, and it sold well and then he said, "So that went well!"

And the next year, he said, "What else would you like to do?"

I said, "I'd like to do one on how to calm down upset customers."

So, I wrote that one and that was 30 years ago and they are still selling and that got me on Oprah and 60 Minutes and other national media from these little books that have now sold over 250,000 copies each.

Ellen: Wow, that's an amazing story. Were the books instrumental in growing your business? I mean, sounds like they were or you feel like they were supplemental to your speaking?

Rebecca: They were supplemental. Even though Budget Rent-a- Car bought 50,000 copies of the customer service book and another telecom bought the sales book as their text for their sales training courses, it didn't really result in a lot of business for me, per se, but it did give me the gravitas to be able to be noticed by Oprah and 60 minutes and the Wall Street Journal and Forbes.com. It created a presence that I wouldn't have had otherwise.

Ellen: How did you end up focusing on leadership?

Rebecca: I knew that it was a popular topic, and when all else is cut, leadership is not. So, I thought, there are, like you said, a bazillion people who talk about leadership, so what is my secret sauce? And I've lived in Silicon Valley for 50 years and have many Silicon Valley clients, so I thought that gives me some credibility that others who just decide to write about it don't have.

So that's when I really started researching Google and Apple and Intel and Pixar and LinkedIn and Survey Monkey and Airbnb -- what are they doing that's different -- that I could put together so that any company could adapt these concepts, any leader could adapt them. And because Silicon Valley has quite the cachet, it was better than leadership lessons from Barstow.

Ellen: I'm curious, because I remember at some point -- because the part of your business that I'm familiar with is Speaker Net News -- maybe even 10 years ago, you did a little bit of a pivot. Now on Sundays, you remind people about the webinar coming up and you used to not do that. And I just saw that you had pivoted to try to market the paying part of that business more. So, I'm just curious about that pivot and any other pivots that you made to increase your income?

Rebecca: Because we interview so many great people like you that one of them had talked about selling things online, and they said, "You know, you've got to remind people, you got to send them at least two mailers."

So that's what we started doing, sending them out a day in advance. And maybe three days in advance. I think that's the rhythm. And then another thing we did was we said, "Where do we really have some gold that is untapped?"

One of our most popular segments pre-COVID was the Travel Tips segment and I went back through the last 10 years of travel tips, ensured they were still accurate and viable, and we had enough of those to make eight e-books on eight topics -- the international travel is the most popular one, all the nuances of traveling internationally with ease and comfort.

Then there's one on luggage and stuff that you should carry with you that makes life easier. And, there's one on getting great deals from hotels and auto rental companies, etc. and there are eight different topics. And they sell individually for $9. But collectively they're $40 or something, we gave them a break.

So, we looked at what do we have that could be redeployed in a different format that would be more consumable? Because people say "I save your Speaker.Net News." Yeah, but you're not going to remember that to go back and search for it. So, we made it easier.

We also put together-- at the time, it was a binder with CDs-- of 10 of our most popular programs on how to start a speaking business, getting a profitable speaking business. So, we took the transcripts, we took the handouts from all of those plus the CDs of them and we sold those online to people who were not already

Speaker.Net News subscribers. They were people who wanted to get in the business but weren't already.

So, we just looked at where we have some assets that aren't being utilized. Can we repackage those into sellable products?

Ellen: We call that repurposing.

Rebecca: Oh, let me let me mention one thing that people send me. We post questions from our readers, and then they agree to send us back the responses they get.

Ellen: You collect them

Rebecca: Yes. We collect them into what's called a compilation, which typically is free on our website. Well, I looked at the Google Analytics one time and noticed that our most hit page from first time visitors was how to be an effective emcee. That was a compilation. So, I said, "Let's monetize this."

So we took off 90% of the tips that were on there; we kept a few of them. And then we put another call out to our readers for updated tips on how to be a great emcee and compiled it into a little e-report. And we sold that for $4.95. I think it's 11 pages long, but it's full of tips from all really experienced people who know how to emcee. And then after a little while, I decided to couple it with a recording. So, I asked somebody who does this to do a teleseminar for us, so then we bundled the e-book with the recording, and every day we get an order for that product, which we've been selling for 10-15 years.

So, you look at not only your assets, which is the first point I made, but now I'm saying, look at what people are drawn to on your site and productize that, how can you monetize that so that they're not just getting all this free stuff, they're actually paying you a little bit for it.

Ellen: Which is a good thing. What changes have been in your business since COVID?

Rebecca: For the Speaker.Net site side, we're doing many more webcasts. So, Zoom versus the teleseminars. People seem to have the time. In the past they have resented if we had a video that made them sit and watch something for which the visuals were really ancillary, they weren't really critical to understanding the content. But now people are so used to sitting in front of their computers watching and being more interactive with them right during call to make it more engaging.

For my own business, I studied lots of ways to create that interactivity and I'm getting much higher ratings than people who just talk at people for 60 minutes or so.

Ellen: So just to close, do you have any suggestions for speakers to find ways to earn income in addition to speaking?

Rebecca: I'd say those two points are really the key ones--to look at what are you what assets do you have that you're not monetizing. And the second one is, what are what are people coming to read on your site already? And how can you turn that into even a $4.95 product, which is more than you were getting before?

And it's such a low price point it's a no brainer.

Ellen: Any anything else you think I forgot to ask?

Rebecca: To look at creating products from their books. Don't just try to sell the book to me. I have 28 books, that's way too many books! You don't look at the book necessarily to be a big moneymaker. But how could you divide that into a 6- or 9- or 10-part master course that then you could sell. Or what are you doing to take that same content but put it in a different format that can yield a higher price.

Ellen: We talked about that in our book, *Authors! The Quick Book to Business Method*. That's a big part of that book. So you're making it full circle, which is quite cool.

Thank you so much, Rebecca. I really appreciate you taking the time.

Chapter Eight

The Art and Science of the Funnel

"Sometimes we make the process more complicated than we need to. We will never make a journey of a thousand miles by fretting about how long it will take or how hard it will be. We make the journey by taking each day step by step and then repeating it again and again until we reach our destination."
~ Joseph B. Wirthlin

In this chapter, we'll discuss the funnel in more detail and show you how you can use it to turn your book into a business. While creating a funnel involves some technology, it isn't difficult, and the processes and concepts are fairly simple.

What is a Funnel?

A funnel is a series of offers.

In the last chapter, we talked about offering something for free when you speak. That's the first offer and it sends the reader to a webpage that you own or control with an opt-in form (sometimes called a sign-up form). As we mentioned earlier, you get the code for the form from your email service provider.

Connie uses Aweber (http://ConnieLoves.me/Aweber) and Ellen uses BirdSend (https://EllenHelps.me/birdsend). This makes creating the opt-in form a fairly simple copy and paste operation. You don't need to understand the code!

The opt-in form serves two important purposes:

It stores the reader's name and email address in your account with your email service provider

When the form is completed, it gives you permission to email the reader

So, you can now set up a system for contacting the reader. You can make further offers in those emails. Later in this book, we'll talk more about how this system works.

Finally, you can make offers on a web page. Readers can get to that web page through a link in an email, after completing the opt-in form, or from a link on social media.

To summarize, you can place offers that are part of your funnel in three places:

- In your talk (or on a slide you display when you speak)
- In emails
- On your website

Types of Offers You Should Make

Which types of offers should you make? Should you promote a product, a free offer, a course, a strategy session, or something else?

In almost all cases, you want to promote a free offer that's related to your talk. The reason for this is that you want to start by getting your readers' email address and the highest chance of doing that is with something for free.

The free offer should have real value and help people with the same problem that your talk solves. It can be a supplement to the talk, such as a workbook or checklist that helps readers implement the content of your talk.

If you're writing fiction, you could create a short guide to the back story of the main characters or a pamphlet telling your own story and how it led to the book.

Here are some other ideas of offers you can make:

- **Related products:** Your products, Private Label Rights products, affiliate products (we'll explain these later in this book)
- **Related services:** Done-for-you services, an assessment, coaching
- **Memberships:** Offering a trial month of a membership at a low price is a great way to get recurring income

Your offer should make clear that subscribers will get emails—give them a clue as to the content and frequency. This provides the clarity required by the General Data Protection Regulation (GDPR), a European Union law that requires transparency and privacy. You can put a short statement to this effect below the opt-in form.

Later in this chapter, I'll explain how you can use offers without an opt-in form.

How to Add an Offer in Your Talk

Let's start by talking about your first offer, the one in your talk.

How do you add an offer when you speak? We gave you some techniques in the last chapter—you just offer a link that goes to a web page you own or control.

Pay attention to the web page you're linking to because you want as many people as possible who get there to complete the form. The percentage of visitors to that page who actually sign up is called the "conversion rate" because you're converting visitors (readers) to subscribers. The page should be:

- Very relevant to the topic of the book and to your readers
- As irresistible (valuable) as possible
- Attractive—use a big image!
- Easy to read

- Simple so that people can skim and get right to the opt-in form

When to Add Offers in Your Talk

When should you make your offer? Well, first of all, you should mention it more than once. And yes, you can have more than one type of offer at different times - some people might be ready to buy right away and others won't - but focus on one main offer. Remember that your main goal is to turn readers into subscribers.

Why should you put the offer in several places? There are several reasons for this.

1) While you certainly wrote your speech to be useful throughout, you'd be surprised how many people don't stay to the end - especially during a webinar. If you leave your offer to the end, some people will never hear it.
2) Readers may need to see and hear an offer several times before they decide to take you up on it. Once you have engaged them and they start to understand your content and appreciate your expertise, they'll be more amenable to giving you their name and email address.

One technique you can use is to start by promising your audience a gift if they stay until the end.

Another technique is to offer a handout that's mainly for taking notes. However, this will only work if you can contact them in advance or they are listening with their computer open and can take notes.

Remember, if you are organizing a webinar, you already have their name and email from their registration.

How Many Offers Should You Have?

However, different people might be interested in different offers and as you cover a variety of topics in your talk, you might find that a variety of offers gets you more subscribers. In this situation, you'll have multiple opt-in forms on multiple web pages that you link to, each sending people to a different list or tag in your email service provider's system.

For example, let's say you're talking about productivity. In your talk, you might cover time management, automation, and outsourcing. So, you could have three free offers:

1) Daily Activity Tracking Form
2) Automation Software Resource List
3) Outsourcing Task List and Resources

In this way, you can attract more subscribers based on which is most interesting to them.

Offers Without an Opt-In Form

Your readers are more likely to complete an opt-in form if they know you a little bit and what better way to help them get to know you but with a video of you speaking about your topic in more detail?

You link to this video at the beginning of each topic in your talk. You tell people what value they'll get from the video. That video is on a page on your website, where you can again make your free offer. But the offer in your talk is just for the free video.

If your video is engaging enough and your free offer is a natural extension of the topic, people will opt in. You can even ask them to do so in the video.

CHAPTER NINE

Continuing Your Relationships Via Email

"Relationships feed on credibility, honesty, and consistency."
~ Scott Borchetta

Let's say that some of your readers opt-in and are now listed as subscribers in your email service provider. What now? You can't email them individually, so you need to set up an automated system. Luckily, email service providers have the tools you need.

The purpose of the emails is to create a relationship with your subscribers so that you can turn them into customers. Never forget that. Let's start with setting up the system and then we'll explain how to use emails to turn readers into buyers.

Setting Up Your Email System

There are many email service providers (ESPs) and of course, some are better than others. You don't need a fancy, expensive one, but you do need one that will make it easy for you to create that relationship with your readers.

Choosing the right email service provider is important. Features to consider are:

- Reliability and deliverability rate
- Service (if you are technically challenged, pay a little extra for phone support)
- Automation features, such as tagging and autoresponders
- Flexibility, so you can choose what happens when a person completes an opt-in form

All modern email service providers have 4 features and you need to understand these well. If you are already familiar with an email service provider, you can skip this section. On the other hand, we've seen that some authors are using older providers or are not using all available features, so you might discover something new!

Subscriber List

As we've been describing, when your readers complete an opt-in form, they end up in a database in your email service provider. While we've mentioned that you generally collect a first name and email address, a database can include more information than that. For example, maybe in your business it's advantageous to collect telephone numbers. On the other hand, the more information you ask for, the less likely people will complete the form. So you need to consider carefully what information to request.

You can segment your subscriber list in several ways. Each offer you have should go to a different segment. Older email service providers use the concept of lists, so that each opt-in form puts subscribers into a different list. Newer ones use the concept of tags, so that each opt-in form assigns a different tag to the subscriber. Some ESPs use both systems. The tag method is more flexible because people can have multiple tags, but either system can work for you. (Subscribers can be on multiple lists, but some ESPs count each instance of a subscriber when they charge you.)

Why is segmenting important? Segmenting lets you send out emails that are appropriate to the interests of your subscribers. To follow the earlier example of people interested in management, automation, and outsourcing, you might want to send different emails to the three groups of people, focusing on their chosen interest.

#1: Broadcast Emails

Of course, all ESPs let you send out "broadcast" emails, which are emails that you choose to send whenever you want. These are not sent automatically, but whenever you decide to email your subscribers. You use broadcast emails for the long-term relationship with your subscribers and to build your business.

We'll discuss broadcast emails a bit later in this chapter.

#2: Opt-in Forms

We've already mentioned that ESPs give you the code for opt-in forms. Here's the general process for creating an opt-in form, although the details vary with the ESP:

1) You create a new opt-in (or sign-up) form. You set the fields (usually first name and email address) that you want to collect.
2) You specify which list or tag subscribers are assigned to.
3) You may design the form, including colors, title, etc. If you're using a page builder in WordPress or have a web designer designing your website, the design may be done on your website rather than in your ESP.
4) You copy the code that the ESP gives you. You may have a choice of JavaScript and HTML code and can try each one to see which works best.
5) You open the page where you want the form to go and display the view where you can put code. In WordPress, this is on the Text tab/mode rather than the Visual tab/mode.
6) You paste the code where you want it to go.

This isn't very hard and your ESP's support can walk you through it.

#3: Autoresponders

Autoresponders are just what they sound like – emails that are sent automatically. They are very powerful in their ability to create relationships with new subscribers, yet many authors do not use them well – if at all!

Setting up autoresponders is different in different ESPs. You'll usually find the settings under a special autoresponder section—autoresponders may be called automation, campaigns, drips, sequences, or something else. There will be a place to create the series of emails that you want new subscribers to get, specify how long to wait between emails (such as a day), and perhaps assign a tag when the autoresponder series is done. Assigning a tag when the autoresponder series is done is important to avoid sending your regular broadcasts to people who are new subscribers and are still getting your initial autoresponders. If you send out a lot of broadcasts, this can be a little overwhelming to new subscribers.

You'll assign the autoresponder series to an opt-in form, so that when people complete the form, the autoresponder series starts automatically.

Those four components of an ESP – subscriber list, broadcast emails, opt-in forms, and autoresponders – are all you need to understand to start turning your audience into customers.

Using Autoresponders to Continue the Funnel

Autoresponders are key to creating valuable relationships with new subscribers and moving them through the funnel. The open rate of autoresponders is very high, much higher than of broadcast emails. That's because the level of interest of new subscribers is very high at the beginning of the relationship.

Here's an example of how you can use autoresponders to create a relationship with new subscribers:

1) Subscribers complete your opt-in form.
2) Subscribers automatically see a "thank-you" page which tells them to watch for an email with the information they requested. If you want, you can put a paid offer on this page—or a video.
3) Subscribers get an email (the first autoresponder) with a link to a web page (the "delivery" page)
4) Subscribers click the link in the email to go to the web page where they can click the link to get the free offer
5) The next day, another autoresponder arrives, asking subscribers if they have any questions and inviting them to reply to you.
6) The following day, another autoresponder arrives with a couple of tips to help them get more out of the free offer (and your talk) and maybe a link to a brief video of you talking about your topic.
7) The day after that, another autoresponder arrives with a discount on a related offer.
8) These autoresponders can go on – it's not uncommon to have 7-15 of them.

Can you see how autoresponders accomplish four things? Here they are:

1) They deliver the promised free offer
2) They create a relationship by linking to a video and asking subscribers to reply to you
3) They help subscribers get more out of the offer - and your talk
4) They make an offer for a product

You can't accomplish all of this without autoresponders!

Using Broadcast Emails for Relationship Building

The other side of ESPs is broadcast emails. As we said, these are emails that you choose to send out at any time to your subscribers and you use them for long-term relationships. Your emails can contain many types of content, but here are some examples:

- **Tips on the topic of your talk:** For example, Ellen has a Daily Hot Tip related to Internet Marketing and succeeding with an online business.
- **A link to your latest blog post:** Your blog is a way for you to show off your expertise on your topic and expand on your book. Your subscribers are interested in this topic, so you should continue to offer them more content. Each blog post should end with a call to action – this can be as simple as asking people to comment or you can make a free or paid offer.
- **Offers for your products or those of others (which would use an affiliate link so you can get a commission):** Some speakers shy away from selling, but if you want a business, you need to make offers!
- **Free offers:** These can be yours or those of others (using an affiliate link so you get a commission)
- **Stories:** You're a speaker, so you know how to tell stories! Your subscribers want to hear about you and what you're doing. They also appreciate stories about others that offer relevant messages.

As long as you regularly make a variety of offers, you'll be able to make money. They key word here is "variety." You can't offer the same one product over and over to the same people. To have enough offers, you may want to add a combination of affiliate marketing (promoting products of others) and creating products with rebrandable content that you purchase (Private Label Rights content).

CHAPTER TEN

Developing Your Business on Your Website

"Your website should be your calling card, or your business front door."
~ James Schramko

Email is only one place where you can create relationships and move new subscribers through your funnel so that they become customers. Email is important because it's where you start the relationship—remember that you gave audience members a link to an opt-in page and they filled out the form to get your free offer. They get that free offer via email.

But perhaps the most obvious place to develop your business is on your website—or a third-party platform. When you're ready to sell, you need a way to accept credit cards and deliver your products or services.

Choosing the Right Selling Platform for Your Business

In order to have a business, you need to be able to sell products from your website or a third-party platform. Before we go into specific options, let's talk about the difference between using your website or a third-party platform. There are also blended options that use both your website and a third-party platform —in fact, these are very common. Let's discuss these options because there are advantages and disadvantages to each.

Selling from your website gives you most control and may be less expensive, depending on your selling platform. It also looks professional to sell directly from your website. But the more control you have, the more responsibility you have and you may find that the technical requirements are too much for you. Of course, you can outsource these tasks.

Getting a Merchant Account and Gateway

You need both a merchant account (to hold the money you make) and a gateway (to process credit cards) but in most cases, you'll get these as a package. The 3 most popular are:

- **PayPal:** This is a merchant account and gateway combination. You'll need a business account. PayPal Payments Standard is easiest but moves buyers to PayPal's website during payment. PayPal Payments Pro requires more technical expertise but keeps buyers on your website. (There's also a monthly charge.) Get more information by visiting the link here. (https://www.paypal.com/us/webapps/mpp/payment-methods) We recommend PayPal for beginners.
- **Stripe:** This is similar to PayPal but may be a little harder for beginners. Stripe is known for great security. Get more information by visiting the link here. (https://stripe.com/US/payments)
- **Authorize.net:** This is a gateway but you can get it bundled with a merchant account that it recommends or use your own.

Choosing a Shopping Cart

You also need a shopping cart to create a "Buy" button on your website. Actually, you can, for example, use a simple PayPal Buy button but your options after that are limited. A shopping cart does several things:

1) Stores product information and displays it to your potential customer
2) Connects with your gateway and merchant account to process the payment
3) Informs you of the sale

4) Connects with your email service provider so you can send your customer an email with product information
5) Redirects buyers to a page of your choice so your customer can download an electronic product

Consider what you need. Do you want to offer recurring products, like a membership program? Do you want to drip content out over time? If you are using a WordPress website, are you OK with using a plug-in that you have to configure and update? Do you want 24/7 phone support? These are all issues that will help determine which solution you choose.

We won't go into great detail here, but here are some solutions for selling from your website:

- A simple PayPal button will give you the fewest options but it's the easiest solution for getting started quickly
- Many people use WooCommerce, a free WordPress plug-in. It has many paid add-ons if you need them.
- Some online options are Zaxaa (https://EllenHelps.me/Zaxaa), Nanacast (http://ConnieLoves.me/Nanacast), and 1ShoppingCart.
- Then there are third-party platforms that don't even require you to have a website, such as JVZoo, WarriorPlus, ClickFunnels, and LeadPages.

Here are considerations for making the right choice:

- Stability, security, and regular updates
- Support
- Ease of use
- Cost
- Features – see the next sections in this chapter for some of the features you might look for

Creating Funnels for Your Business

Once you have the sales infrastructure in place, you need to create your funnels. Unless you use one of the third-party platforms, you'll create your funnels on your website. Either way, you can create simple or complex funnels. Start with simple ones until:

- You see what works for your audience
- You learn the process

It's very important to put yourself in your reader's shoes and think of all the possible entry points into your funnel. For example, someone who hasn't heard you speak may come to a blog post on your website and opt in for your freebie. On the other hand, someone who has heard you speak may hear your offer for your freebie and opt-in having already heard your talk. Do you see how you have to allow for people to come from various places and move them through the funnel in a meaningful way?

We've already discussed the 3 places to put offers:

- Your talk (whether you speak out an opt-in page URL, give them a sheet of paper, or some other method)
- Your emails
- Your website

In the next chapter, we'll explain how creating a course based on your speech is the natural next step in your funnel. And we've explained the technology of creating an opt-in form and a sales button. With all of that clear, let's look at some possible funnels that will turn your speech into a thriving business.

1) **Speech to freebie to course:** This is the most obvious funnel for speakers who want to create a business from their speaking. In your speech, you make an offer to a freebie with a link to the opt-in page. Then, in the freebie, you make an offer for a course based on the speech.

2) **Email to freebie to speech to course:** This assumes that you send an email to your subscribers offering them a freebie (which you might derive from your speech). In the freebie, you make an offer for your speech—it can be a live talk or something you have pre-recorded. (If it's online, it could be called a webinar, masterclass, or video.) When you speak, you make an offer for the related course.
3) **Blog post to freebie to speech to course:** This is like the previous funnel except that you write a blog post and promote it. Some people might find it by searching, too. In the blog post, you promote your freebie. In the freebie, you make an offer for your speech. In the speech, you make an offer for the related course. Or, you could promote your speech in your blog post and from there, funnel #1 would work.
4) **Email to speech to course:** In this funnel, you promote your speech in an email. From there, people can find your freebie or your course.

Just remember that your speech can be live in person, live online, or pre-recorded.

The first contact can come from anywhere – joint venture partners, organic search on the Internet, ads, social media posts, and, of course, email.

Do you see that because you don't know where everyone will start, you need to make offers everywhere? So, your speech should include an offer for both your freebie and your course. Either way, readers will end up on your email list so you can make further offers and expand your business.

More about Funnels-Bumps, Upsells, and Downsells

Funnels can get sophisticated. When a person subscribes for your freebie, make an offer for your speech or course on the thank-you/download page.

A sales funnel can include bumps, upsells, and downsells. In order to create these, your selling platform needs to offer them as a feature. These are somewhat advanced, so first get your main funnels working before trying these. Here are some helpful definitions:

- **Bump:** This is like "Do you want fries with that?" On the sales page, BEFORE a person clicks the Buy button, there's a checkbox that adds a low-priced addition. For example, you might add templates when a person buys a book from you.
- **Upsell:** Upsells comes AFTER the purchase. Before people get access to the product, they see another sales page that adds to the original product. They either click the Buy button or choose "No thanks."
- **Downsell:** Downsells also come AFTER the purchase and happen when a person chooses "No thanks" for an upsell or simply abandons a sales page or sales cart page. The downsell will be lower in price than the upsell or original product.

CHAPTER ELEVEN

Using Social Media to Grow Your Business

"Content is fire. Social media is gasoline."
~ Jay Baer

Social media platforms offer you many opportunities for promoting your speaking and your business. You can reach many people without cost, although you can reach more people if you buy ads. Here are some pointers for using social media effectively.

Creating Relationships on Social Media

To succeed in promoting your speaking and your business on social media, you need to be social! That means you need to systematically increase the number of your friends, contacts, and followers.

While you can - and should - automate posting on social media, you also need to be there in person for the personal touch. This means responding to comments on your posts and liking the posts of others.

Using Social Media Strategically

Social media can take you "down the rabbit hole" so be careful to use it strategically. Don't socialize for the sake of socializing. Get in, create a post, and get out. Look at your notifications and don't spend much time at all on your timeline or main feed.

Groups are also extremely valuable because they are organized around an interest. Join groups that contain people in your target market and post in them. Just be sure to follow the rules that are posted in that group.

Making Offers on Social Media

Because social media is supposed to be social, you shouldn't just make offers all the time. Instead, you need to balance your posts with:

- Free information, including your blog posts, posts and articles of others, etc.
- Inspirational content to help others
- Your offers

When you find someone who seems to need your help, it's usually best to do a private message so that the conversation is personal. You can create some valuable relationships this way with not only potential customers but potential partners.

Connie teaches an ongoing live course on how to use social media to syndicate your content, build relationships, and sell more online. This program is called Syndication Optimization and you may benefit from being a part of this.

PART III

Moving Forward with Speaking as an Income Stream

"There are three things to aim at in public speaking: first, to get into your subject, then to get your subject into yourself, and lastly,
to get your subject into the heart of your audience."
~ Alexander Gregg

In Part III we'll take a look at the fear of public speaking and ways to overcome that so you may begin to move forward. Then we will discuss the concept of embracing the "speak to business" model for your business.

Chapter 13 is about your willingness to "put yourself out there" with your speaking. The art of delivering your speech in person is the focus of Chapter 14. Then we move on to the concept of "What's for Sale?" and "Selling from the Stage" in Chapters 15 and 16, respectively.

Chapter 17 is all about speaking online, whether you are selling or not.

CHAPTER TWELVE

Putting Yourself Out There

"The most powerful person in the world is the storyteller. The storyteller sets the vision, values and agenda of an entire generation that is to come."
~ Steve Jobs

There were so many stories I longed to share with others, but my fear of speaking held me back for years. I was too afraid to speak in front of people for several reasons, including lack of confidence and low self-esteem. That's why I had to overcome this fear and decided to turn public speaking into an action that would become a part of my DNA. I had been saying no to opportunities that were destined to broaden my horizons and this had to change. I thought of what former first lady Eleanor Roosevelt had said so many years ago...

"You must do the thing you think you cannot do."

It was 2006 and I had just arrived in my new city. After resigning from my job as a classroom teacher at the end of the school year, as well as giving away my best real estate clients to others who could better serve them, I decided to relocate as part of my life reinvention. I was ready to start my new business on the internet. Within a couple of weeks, I came to the realization that working from home was going to be a lonely proposition.

This led to a search for volunteer opportunities in my new community. The international service organization Rotary held weekly meetings. I showed up to see what it was all about. Soon they asked me to do a talk on this new internet business I had been telling them about. I was scared to death but knew they were supportive of my endeavors and wanted to do more online with their own businesses. On that hot and humid day in

August of 2006 my speaking career was launched in front of sixty Rotarians at the Marie Callender's restaurant next to the freeway on ramp to Interstate 5, about fifty miles north of Los Angeles.

This led to speaking engagements for the local Chamber of Commerce and the Rotary District event in downtown Los Angeles, where there were three hundred people in attendance. I was still so scared each time I got up on stage. My heart would pound and my stomach did flip flops in the minutes leading up to my turn on stage. I prayed for the confidence to be able to comfortably speak in front of groups of any size and it would be a full two years before that occurred.

It was in Minneapolis, Minnesota in June of 2008 that I had been asked by legendary marketer Armand Morin to speak at his annual event. I passed him in the hallway on my way to the conference room, where he asked me if I was nervous.

"I'm nervous because I am not nervous this time," I answered. He laughed and smiled.

When I got up on stage the nerves crept back in. I assumed this would be another time where my mouth would get dry. I would read most of the slides, making very little eye contact with anyone in the audience. My fear of speaking was an unwelcome visitor.

But something happened that I cannot explain. It began when I said something funny and a few people laughed. Then I said something else and I was building rapport with the group. I sailed through my presentation, interacted by answering a few questions, and sold several copies of the program I was offering.

It was a feeling I can only describe as one in which I was empowered and confident in knowing that I had information and knowledge that would be of benefit to others when I shared it. In those moments on stage, I had promised myself I would never forget how this felt. I had wanted this feeling and experience so badly and now it had arrived. It was as though a gift had been bestowed on me and my light was shining more brightly. And I now knew I could call myself a public speaker and change my life forever.

The next day I once again thought about Eleanor Roosevelt. She had also said,

"Do one thing every day that scares you."

These days I speak virtually and in person on a regular basis. My goal is to seek out different venues in which to speak and to connect with more people from a variety of backgrounds and life experiences. Scaring myself has become something of a hobby. It's my way of measuring how much I am growing as a human. Sharing my message with others is a gift for which I will be eternally grateful.

Doing the thing I thought I could not do is changing my life.

Embracing the "Speak to Income" Model

I've already shared many stories here of how I began as a speaker. I'd like to elaborate on that now and take you from where I was in 2004 up until the point where I first realized that public speaking was a part of my income model and that I had, first by accident and then with full knowledge and intention created an online stream of revenue directly related to speaking on my topics of influence and interest.

For twenty years I worked as a classroom teacher in the inner city of Los Angeles, California. Simultaneously, I ran a small real estate company where I was what is referred to as the "responsible" broker and after 1989, also a certified residential real estate appraiser. Throughout this time, I was living a life of mediocrity. You may recall from the second chapter of this book that I shared Les Brown's goal of wanting to deliver "a message that would help people become uncomfortable with their mediocrity." I was one of those people. Allow me to elaborate on this line of thinking...

Your Defining Moment as a Speaker

Once I saw with my own eyes the transformation that could occur once someone stepped on to a stage and uttered a few words I knew my life could change, and very quickly.

The year was 2004 and I had just returned from a six month leave of absence from my teaching job at the beginning of the year. The principal at the school had called me in to her office and told me she would be leaving the long-term substitute in my classroom through the end of the school year in June.

She paused for dramatic effect and waited until I said the first words.

"If Mr. Carter will be in my room, where will I be every day?"

Again, she hesitated for a moment before answering my question.

"I'm assigning you as the Psychomotor teacher. And when you're not on the yard you'll be helping the teachers with math and language arts in their classrooms. I expect a complete lesson plan with details to be given directly to me every Monday morning as soon as you have clocked in."

You could have knocked me over with a feather. After I had worked so hard to overcome a serious work injury with surgery and physical therapy, in addition to undergoing treatments for a major illness during these past six months, I would now be on the playground supervising large groups of children every day. Later it would be revealed that I would be alone as the sole adult during these days on the schoolyard.

My school fell under the Title I legislation which required meetings by track and grade level each week, and someone had to be in charge of the children during this time. Typically, it was a substitute teacher or one of our regular teachers during their off-track (we were a four track, year around school) time, but now it would be me.

Not wanting for her to see how I truly felt, I answered her quickly.

"Thank you, Mrs. Kravitz. I look forward to working with the students and the other teachers in this way. I appreciate your confidence in me."

I was not being flippant, cavalier, or sarcastic. I honestly believed I could do this job and do it well. My survival depended on it because I needed this job, along with the paycheck and medical insurance that came along with it.

On the way home that day I stopped at a sporting goods store and purchased a green lanyard and a shiny metal whistle. I wasn't happy but I was determined to make it through until the end of the school year. Once at home I took my wall calendar down so I could count the days. There were one hundred seventy-eight days until the end of June. I took a black marker and placed an "X" over the box for January the 2nd and sat down on my sofa. It was Friday night and I would need at least a couple of hours of television and some chocolate to get over this day.

On Monday I showed up at school very early, as I always did. I was usually the second person on campus each day, arriving just a few minutes after the school's custodian. Although I had the key to the classroom on my key chain, that wasn't my room any longer. I sat in my car until the office manager arrived and then waited on the bench in the entryway until Mrs. Kravitz came in. Using only her head she motioned me into her office and shut the door loudly behind me as I sat down.

"Have you had time to think about what I said, Mrs. Green?"

Yes, I had and I was prepared for this moment.

"It was a wonderful weekend. Mrs. Kravitz. I did some research and printed out some things so I'll be able to start this morning."

I stood up and handed her the notebook I had stuffed into the side of my purse. She turned each page slowly, examining the lesson plans and Education Code information I had printed out. After three pages she slammed the notebook shut and placed it on the edge of her desk so that I would have to get up to retrieve it. Our conversation was over.

She had called a staff meeting for immediately after school. I spent the day figuring out things like where to keep my purse and lunch all day if I didn't have a classroom or an office. I also spoke with the after-school coach when he arrived after lunch, and with three teachers during their recess and lunch breaks. Then I spent some time speaking with Mr. Carter, the long-term substitute who would be finishing out the school year in my classroom with my students.

As everyone began showing up in the auditorium for the staff meeting, I chose a seat near the front door. Many people were happy to see that I had returned after my six-month absence; others didn't say a word and kept on moving towards their seats.

At exactly three fifteen Mrs. Kravitz called the meeting to order. After a couple of announcements, she turned to me and motioned for me to stand up. All eyes were on me as she said,

"Today we're welcoming Mrs. Green back to our school. She will be assuming the role of Psychomotor teacher through the end of the school year. Also, Mr. Carter will remain in Room 23 through the end of this school year. Mrs. Green, why don't you say a few words to the faculty."

That moment was a turning point in my life. I was already standing, as the principal had instructed me to do earlier. I had unknowingly selected a seat close to the front of the auditorium, and now I was positioned perfectly to step into my power and speak my message to the sixty or so people in front of me.

Stepping into Your Power as a Speaker

I won't tell you what I said on that day, even though it is as clear in my memory as if it had occurred yesterday. Instead, I will tell you how I felt and the impact it had, both on my life and in my career from that day forward.

I took a step forward at some point before I began speaking, and paused for a nanosecond to feel the energy in the room. I became aware of feet shuffling and someone coughing and I sensed the awkward uneasiness of my audience.

For the three minutes or so I had the undivided attention of the people in that auditorium, I was in complete control - of my emotions, of their emotions, and of my future. Parts of my life flashed in front of me while I spoke and I knew I could never go back to being the person I had been for way too many years. My tiny step forward was a giant leap for me and for all people who have struggled to be heard and to take control over their lives, at that moment and throughout history.

As I closed, I smiled broadly and thanked everyone in the room for their kindness and support while I had been out for six months on medical leave. And then I turned to Mrs. Kravitz and thanked her for believing in me. I spoke my final words, leaving all of the people in the auditorium with my heartfelt promise, and that was to perform my duties as the new psychomotor teacher to the best of my abilities and to ask for ongoing support and feedback to make our program one of the best ones in the district. I thanked them once again and slowly turned as I took my seat.

A few people far in the back of the auditorium clapped, someone cheered, and there was a wave of loud whispers and rumbling. I had stepped up and put my reputation on the line. On that day, Connie Ragen Green became a public speaker and I could never go back, nor would I ever want to return to being the person I once had been.

Always Be Prepared

Years ago, I attended a live event in Houston, Texas. It was a three-day marketing event with four speakers each day. Right before the end of our lunch break on the first day the event's organizer came up to the group of people I was speaking with and announced that one of the speakers would be unable to attend. He was having an issue with customs and they were not allowing him to board his plane. This was truly a dilemma and one that had to be dealt with immediately.

Out of the corner of my eye I could see someone walking nonchalantly up to our group. He had something in his hand and he laid it flat in his outstretched right palm as he said,

"I have two presentations ready. One is on increasing sales conversions through copywriting and the other is more general about online business, with an emphasis on writing sales copy."

We were all quiet, waiting in anticipation to see what the organizer would say. Without hesitation he answered,

"The one on copywriting will work. Thanks, Ray."

The man was legendary copywriter Ray Edwards and he taught all of us a valuable lesson that day. We must always be ready to speak. Keeping a thumb drive with you wherever you go is the fastest method of carrying your slide presentations with you.

It's interesting to note that several years later I had invited Ray to speak at an event in Atlanta. When I spoke with the event organizer, he mentioned that he had scheduled Ray to present in one of the breakout rooms. This surprised me and I asked to speak with him alone. After a short discussion he agreed that it would be better to have Ray deliver a presentation at the end of each day's keynotes.

"But he's on the plane flying in right now. He won't have any time to put together a different presentation before we begin in the morning," he said.

"Don't worry. He'll have several for you to choose from," I answered. Ray did and brought down the house with his talk.

A mentor told me later that it's best to have two presentations ready, one that can be delivered in about an hour to ninety minutes and another, shorter one that can be delivered in twenty to thirty minutes. I have done this for almost a decade now and change up the two presentations once a year to make sure my material is fresh and relevant.

Rotary International and Toastmasters Join Forces

At the beginning of 2020 an alliance was announced between Rotary International and Toastmasters. Rotary is an international service organization with more than 1.2 million members in over two hundred countries. I have been a member since 2006 and credit this group with helping me to become a public speaker.

I had heard about the group Toastmasters over the years, primarily from people I worked with in real estate. They would tell stories of being able to practice their "listing pitches" so they could do this more effectively at our local meetings. I began to watch these people and came to the conclusion they were very good speakers who were able to get their points across, effortlessly and succinctly.

Other than that observation I gave little thought to Toastmasters. I was a classroom teacher and also worked in real estate, most often as a residential appraiser and listing broker. I honestly believed that public speaking was not an important skill for me to practice. And I also knew that I had a fear of speaking that I did not want to acknowledge or address at that point in time.

Fast forward to 2006 and my life has shifted significantly, by my own choice. When I resigned from my job as a classroom teacher and gave away my best real estate clients, I moved to a new city about thirty miles north of where I had been living for fourteen years previously. Overnight I was thrust into a world that took place on the internet and required me to be in front of my computer for at least six hours each day. In addition, I had built a new home in a semi-rural area of my new city and there were only a dozen or so homes already built and occupied when I arrived. The result was that I began to feel very isolated. This surprised me because I am an introvert and believed that the solitude would suit me. I was learning so much about myself during this time and decided to get out and see what the city had to offer.

I first discovered Rotary, an international service organization whose primary projects include bringing fresh water to locations where that is an issue and eradicating polio from our planet. Even though I was intimidated by the people I met on my first visit, I decided to make that a part of my learning experience and continued to attend the meetings and to get involved with volunteering for their local projects. I enjoyed the fellowship as well as the weekly speakers they brought to our group.

Early on they had a speaker who shared the details of a local scholarship fund. It was only at the end of her talk that she thanked Rotary for giving members of the local Toastmasters the opportunity to practice their speaking.

On that day I decided that my logical next step was to visit the local Toastmasters chapter which met two evenings a month. Now remember that I shared earlier that I am an introvert. Actually, I am an extreme introvert. Even though it was my very first meeting and I wasn't sure what to expect, my imagination worked overtime to scare me. It turned out everyone was very nice and I did go for a few meetings, but ultimately, I did not join Toastmasters.

I did join my local Rotary and soon they began thrusting the microphone into my hands to talk about an upcoming project. In the beginning I would stand up and look at my shoes for the entire thirty seconds I was speaking. Then I would thrust out my hand and someone, unknown to me because I still hadn't looked up would take the microphone and I would sit down. For the next several minutes my face and ears felt hot and I couldn't hear what anyone was saying because I was experiencing so much fear. And each time I told myself that I would never do it again.

Later on, I would think about the people who were telling me that becoming a public speaker would open doors for me. My counter was always that I didn't want those doors to open, but as time passed I knew that was exactly what I wanted and needed to grow my business. So, each time I saw the microphone coming towards me so I could share with my fellow Rotarians what projects we were working on and those that were upcoming, I welcomed the opportunity to be so scared my heart would feel like it was jumping out of my chest.

I began speaking regularly at Rotary on various topics related to my new business. Each Club around the world needs a speaker to present a program approximately forty weeks each year. Soon they recommended me to the Program Director for our District and he invited me to speak to a group of over three hundred people. This was a new beginning for me and finally I understood what people had meant when they had told me that speaking would open doors for me.

When I published my first book in the early summer of 2010, I dedicated it to my Rotary Club and to Rotary District 5260 of which I was a part. These people became a part of my village as I had grown as an author, entrepreneur, and finally a speaker.

The fact that Rotary is now collaborating with Toastmasters warms my heart. I believe this will provide opportunities for Rotarians to become public speakers more easily and with training. My goal is to inspire people who may be interested in a life of public speaking to get involved with service organizations in order to reach their full potential.

Procuring Speaking Engagements

Speakers speak. If you are to become proficient with your speaking, and with your ability to earn income based on speaking to others on your topic you must seek out venues where you will be in front of others, virtually or in person on a regular basis.

I have already mentioned Rotary as an organization that needs speakers on a regular basis to present at their weekly meetings. There are also a number of groups who are also seeking out speakers. My recommendation is to go online and look for your community's calendar of events. Attend some of these that are of interest to you and find out what they are about. Even if you find that a group is not a good fit for you, there is still an opportunity to connect with people and let them know more about you and what you have to offer. And attend some meetings that may seem at first to not be of interest to you. You could be pleasantly surprised if you are willing to get out of your comfort zone.

Be willing to invest the time to get to know people and organizations in your community. Many people visit Rotary or another group once or twice and do not go back again. Relationship building takes time and is worth your effort. It was several years before another Rotarian recommended me as a corporate consultant. That led to a new career within my online business that might not have ever opened up to me if I hadn't been willing to be a part of Rotary and several other groups over the years.

CHAPTER THIRTEEN

Delivering Your Speech in Person

"Listening happens when we put in
the effort to understand what it means.
It not only requires focus, but also a commitment
to encountering the intent and emotion behind the words."
~ Seth Godin

No matter how much preparation you have given to learning about the history of speaking, choosing a topic, defining your goals, and putting together your signature speech, there is nothing that can quite prepare you for stepping on to the stage and delivering your talk to a live audience, be it in person or virtually. And the energy you receive from speaking in front of a group is impossible to describe.

But the physical experience of delivering your speech is actually the second part of the speaking process. It all begins the moment your speech has been completely written, rewritten, edited, and you have rehearsed it out loud at least one hundred times.

A hundred times?! What?! Wait, don't go. I can feel you closing this book or turning off your tablet as your eyes scan my words in disbelief. Please come back...

Preparation is crucial to success in life. I learned that long ago when I spent three full months preparing for the Spelling Bee in fifth grade. I easily won by beating out the reigning champion for the previous five years. I revisited that memory in 2009 when I entered the "Better Your Best" contest for improving my business. I committed fully to spending time every single day for many months to help ensure I could walk away with the 25K cash grand prize.

Allow me to explain how this contest worked. First, you had to be a part of Armand Morin's AM^2 Mastermind. The "squared" part of AM^2 represented the partnership Armand had with Alex Mandossian at that time.

Once you were a part of this Mastermind you were eligible to apply for their annual "Better Your Best" contest. They got the name from Joe Polish, a thought leader and marketer who had hosted his own contests over the years. In 2002 Joe started "Better Your Best" and when he discussed this with Armand, they decided that each of them would do this on an annual basis in order to help the people they mentored to reach their full potential.

The purpose of entering was to share how you had improved your business during the previous year and to show the results. Everything had to be documented and recorded and then submitted to the team of six hand-picked judges for further examination. The judges each had one vote and then the audience would hear each contestant speak on the final night and the votes would be tabulated and then count as one additional vote. I had heard stories that over the years the judges had been deadlocked at a tie vote, and that it was the cumulative audience vote that tipped the scales in the direction of the winner.

Another thing I will add here is that the amount of money you earned from your business was not a factor, so if someone earned a million dollars from a well marketed launch that would not have any bearing on the decision of the judges.

I first observed how the contest worked when I attended Armand's "Big Seminar" in the spring of 2008. I was not yet a member, but did make the decision to join by the end of that life changing weekend.

On Friday evening the event attendees were invited back into the ballroom after dinner. Seven contestants took the stage and one after another they were given four minutes to speak to the audience and share everything they wanted us to know about them and their business.

At the time I honestly believed I would never be a part of something like this. My confidence was not very strong and my self-esteem was just beginning to blossom. And my business was growing, slowly but steadily but I didn't feel like anything I was doing was important enough to share with the world in a contest. And that is why I paid little attention to what each contestant said during their four-minute speech or how they conveyed their message. Public speaking just wasn't on my radar at that time.

Six months into Armand's Mastermind and I had changed my mind about entering the contest. Looking back at this point in time, I'm not exactly sure what motivated me to come to the realization that I was "Better Your Best" material. It could have been a number of things, but if I had to pinpoint one particular moment in time that I began to believe in myself it would have to be when Dr. Jeanette Cates, a founding member of AM² told me that what I was doing in my online business was unique and innovative and should be shared with others.

Having someone believe in you makes a difference in your life. When it is someone you have looked up to and followed for years the difference it makes is incalculable. Jeanette and I are still friends and colleagues to this day and her wisdom and insight never ceases to amaze me. She even agreed to write the Foreword for this book and you probably read it when you first got your copy and looked through the beginning pages.

I worked diligently for many months to prepare for this contest. At a certain point in the process, you had to submit a physical package showing everything you had done to improve your business during the allotted time. My package definitely had the "thud" factor as I carted it into the post office to send to Armand's offices in North Carolina. Within a few weeks I was notified that I had been selected as one of five finalists. I was over the moon with this announcement.

The final step in the process would come more than a month later. At that time, we would once again be at the Big Seminar. It was held at the M Hotel in Las Vegas in November of 2009. I arrived a day early to meet up with the people I already knew, as well as those from my online community I had invited to attend that weekend. They were excited to support me in this way and I felt more confident having them there.

On Thursday afternoon I ventured into the ballroom to see who was there and to take a closer look at the stage. I was met by George Callen, Armand's right-hand man and someone who had become a dear friend over the past year. He greeted me with a big hug and a handshake and congratulated me on making it to the finals. There would be five of us in all and I knew each person because of the relationships we had built in the Mastermind.

George went back to what he had been working on and I made my way up to the stage. As I took each step to the top, I paused to express my gratitude for being a part of this experience. And as much as I wanted to win the "Better Your Best" contest I knew down deep inside that I was already a winner for making it this far. I never take anything in my life for granted and take full responsibility for making great things happen.

The Big Seminar began on Friday morning. Armand was the opening speaker and he mentioned the contest almost right away. He had each of the finalists stand up as he mentioned our name and said a few words about us. I wish I hadn't been so nervous and could remember now what he said about me.

After dinner we met back in the ballroom and the five of us competing in the contest made our way up to the stage. There were five high back chairs waiting for us. Armand's wife,

Marianna was given the task of assigning each of us in the queue. I was third. We were given exactly four minutes to speak to the audience. There was a large red timer in the back of the room that counted down to zero. The rule was that if you went over your time you would be disqualified. I had practiced at least a hundred times and knew I would have about fifteen seconds left at the end of my presentation.

I cannot remember much about what the other finalists said, but I do recall that they each used a slide presentation as they spoke. When it was my turn the person running the projector asked for my slides. I reminded him that I did not have any and would not need the projector.

The timer started and I stepped up to the microphone. I spent a few seconds taking in the moment and looking out over the sea of more than three thousand people in attendance. Then I began to speak...

When you look out into the audience from the stage at an event of this size the lights are so bright you can barely make out who is in front of you past the front row. But I did spot several of the people who had come to cheer me on that weekend. One was Cynthia, one of my first clients and someone I am proud to call a friend. As the timer counted down it was Cynthia who began to panic. I could see her motioning to me to hurry up and finish. Because I had practiced exactly what I was going to say over and over and over again I knew my timing was spot on. I shared my last words with the audience, closing with "Thank you. My name is Connie Ragen Green." There were eight seconds remaining as I stepped away from the microphone and into the shadows. The audience gave me a standing ovation but I wasn't sure I had won until Armand announced it at the very end of the presentations.

Your Words Have Great Power

Remember that the spoken word was the first communication between early humans. When you speak out loud you are bringing forth your inner spirit that comes from a place of power deep inside of you and is imprinted in your DNA.

A speech can affect people deeply and bring about great change and evolution on a personal level. Your speaking can also bring about a shift in the thinking of masses of people and even start a movement. An example of this occurred when Dr. Martin Luther King Jr gave his "I Have a Dream" speech on the 28th day of August in 1963.

I have seen this occur in one of the cities where I live, Santa Clarita, California after the high school shooting incident on November 14th, 2019. Students and teachers from the school, as well as community leaders brought about healing and change through the words they spoke. This provided unforeseen opportunities for young people to have a voice in sharing how this tragedy changed their lives forever and I watched firsthand as leaders were born. Teachers, parents, and first responders also showed up as they stepped in front of the microphone and allowed the world to hear them speak their innermost thoughts on what had occurred.

More recently, people speaking out about the COVID-19 pandemic and during the "Black Lives Matter" protests affected millions of people with the power of their words. These messages are coming straight from the heart and based on centuries of experiences that are now coming to the forefront of our society. My hope is that the words will land in the way in which they are intended and true growth and change for all of us can be attained.

Fear Diminishes the Power of Your Presentation

When it comes to public speaking fear can and will get in the way of your delivering the most impactful presentation you are capable of delivering. Whether you still have a fear around speaking publicly or if you have moved past the fear and on to working on your delivery, I'd like to share some insights with you that will make a difference.

Most speakers I see in person or on a virtual call tend to rush through their slides or handout much too quickly, I believe. As soon as the moderator or host introduces them, they are off to the races and it appears to the audience members that they want it to be over as soon as possible. This does not work in your favor in terms of your credibility. And if you will be offering something for sale at the of your presentation, or even if you will just be sending people to your blog or website to join your list and download a free report or other gift, slow down for best results.

Perhaps you are naturally a fast talker. Slow down. You want your audience to hear and understand and take in every word. People will also trust you more and have a better overall perception of you as an expert in your field if you are willing to speak with authority and take a breath between sentences or bullet points on your slides.

Enjoy the process of speaking, to the point that you are looking forward to spending as much time as you have been allotted to share your message. Pausing between your thoughts spoken aloud give people time to think about what you are saying and to form their own ideas and absorb new or abstract ideas you wish to share with them. Your words will paint a picture and punctuate the meaning you wish to convey. It also gives you time to think, evaluate how your message is landing, and resume your speech.

Rapid speaking also denotes a level of fear and insecurity in the person speaking and can possibly bring about a feeling of distrust to the person listening. You certainly do not want to project that image to those who have come to listen to you speak. Speaking evokes emotion and you want to have control of your own emotions to best evoke powerful thoughts and feelings from those who are hearing you.

Just as music is the sound we hear in between the notes, our speaking voice is best heard and absorbed during the silence we allow between our words and phrases. I believed this concept is misunderstood by most public speakers.

The goal is to teach the people in your audience as much as possible about your topic. Too many times I have come home empty-handed because the speaker went so fast, made a quick pitch at the end, and then left the event before I had any time to ask questions and find out more. Someone who is a seasoned public speaker in the area of finance and investment did this several years ago and I ended up not purchasing a program for several thousand dollars that I was interested in knowing more about on that day. What a shame.

Another thing to consider is something I have already discussed; practice leads to excellence!

I have just shared the story of how I practiced a 4-minute speech over a hundred times before delivering it onstage in front of three thousand people in November of 2009. I was one of five finalists in a contest called "Better Your Best" where we were asked to share how we had improved our businesses from one year to the next. I entered the competition with my eye on the prize (it was 25 thousand dollars in cash!) and I knew my public speaking fear and lack of experience would work against me. One way to practice and improve your speaking pace is to record your presentation on video or audio.

Then listen to it over and over until you can be objective about the areas you will need to work on changing.

Once you have worked through any issues that you discover look for ways to practice speaking publicly as often as possible. I have spoken to groups of as few as five people who gave me excellent feedback on what I had shared. I have also spoken to groups of several hundred to two thousand audience members where my goal, in addition to teaching and sharing as much information as possible was to be well received so that I could sell my programs from the stage and at the back of the room, and also to be asked back and to be referred to other groups looking for public speakers.

I have spoken to non-profits and charitable organizations, community groups, Chambers of Commerce, private clubs, religious groups, real estate groups, and local networking groups as a way to stay sharp for the audiences of authors, speakers, and entrepreneurs that tend to receive my message in a way that resonates with my experience and core values. I almost never say no to any group that needs a public speaker and enjoy the challenge of connecting with new people. And every once in a while, someone will come up to me afterward and share their experiences and challenges, and then I know why I was meant to speak on that particular day.

You may also want to set up a makeshift video studio in your home office or extra bedroom. Don't just let it sit there; practice makes for excellence, so practice! Also, begin to make offers at various price points to be more inclusive with new prospects and ongoing customers and clients.

Set up funnels that lead prospects through the products, courses, and programs you have to offer. And above all else, make sure everyone within shouting distance knows you are a public speaker. Fear of connecting with others will not ever serve you well.

And if your public speaking fear quotient is too high when you are speaking, promoters will smell the fear and not ask you back for a returning speaking engagement in the future.

You can do this and I believe in you! Start small and work your way up to closer to where you would like to be as a public speaker. Keep at it and success will find you.

Authority and Your Power Precept

"If you wish to be perceived as an authority, become an author.
*If you want to **be** the authority,*
speak regularly on your topic."
~ Connie Ragen Green

Authors write, speak, and present themselves as authorities and experts on their topic. We create authority with everything we say, write, and do. The combination of your voice, your words, and your presence comes together to become your story.

I think of this as a 3-part process where your goal is to:

- Speak with passion
- Write with vision
- Carry yourself with conviction

I show up for either a virtual or in person presentation with what I refer to as a "Power Precept." Mine is that I believe anyone can become an entrepreneur if they are willing to learn, implement, and do the work.

Our power precept for this book is that speaking and sharing your message with the world will transform you into a respected authority on your topic, and one that can be turned into an ongoing revenue stream.

I also stand or sit up in a "Power Stance." Stand straight and tall with conviction!

I always speak using my "Power Voice." Think before speaking and look directly into people's eyes while you share what you have to say. Speak with passion!

Finally, I share my "Power Statement." This is a statement that defines you and your core beliefs and values. Here's mine...

"Do for a year what others won't; live forever the way others can't."

I wrote that statement with a vision of my future!

I often stand in the doorways of any place I go to replicate my "Power Stance." This requires you to stand up straight and tall. You want your feet to be equal distance apart and facing forward. Put your weight on the outside edges of each foot and make sure your heels are solid on the floor. This will make a difference, I promise.

When people come up to speak with me, I smile, shake their hand, and listen to what they have to say. When I answer I used my "Power Voice." This means speaking in a confident and deliberate way, maintaining eye content and speaking in a steady and even tone.

And when people ask me to repeat my "Power Statement" I'm prepared to say it slowly and clearly so they may write it down. See if you can imagine me saying...

"Do for a year what others won't; live forever the way others can't."

Try this strategy on for size and feel the power of having your own Power Precept working in your favor.

CHAPTER FOURTEEN

What's for Sale?

"Don't find customers for your products,
find products for your customers."
~ Seth Godin

In order for you to consider turning your speaking into a viable income stream, there must be something for sale. This may appear to be a simple and straightforward statement, but my experience shows that is not the case.

The first time I attended the NAMS (Novice to Advanced Marketing Systems) conference, held in Atlanta, Georgia it was 2011. This was also where I met Ellen, the co-author for this book, for the first time in person. I had invited more than twenty people in my online community to attend and planned a special group event for them the day before the larger conference was to begin.

We sat in a semicircle and initially I had each person introduce themselves by giving their name, where they lived, the name of their business, and the URL of their website.

Next, I asked them to go around the room again and share what their biggest challenge was in terms of building their business. Almost every single person stated that the most difficult thing was earning income.

I then asked for a show of hands to see where they were financially and was surprised to learn that most everyone in the group had earned far less than they had spent during the previous twelve months.

My next question to them was this:

"How many links do you have up online, where someone could make a purchase of one of your products, courses, or services, or that of someone else through your affiliate link without meeting you face to face?"

This time I was shocked to learn that some had zero links out on the internet and most had fewer than ten places where someone could buy from them.

When I announced that I had, at that time more than two thousand links online, they stared at me in disbelief and asked me to explain how I had done this and how they could do the same.

Where was the disconnect here? Why had a concept that seemed to me to be so obvious and elementary in nature completely eluded this group of intelligent and savvy people? I knew they couldn't be alone; my guesstimate is that more than half of the people who start an online business as an author, speaker, and/or an entrepreneur do not make this connection between being in business and having something for sale. Let's explore this further...

The Brick-and-Mortar Business Model

Imagine yourself at the local mall, or on the main street in your community's business district where there are a variety of businesses. These might include clothing stores, restaurants, specialty shops, professional's offices, and more. Now, think about what each one would have for sale.

The restaurants would have a variety of food items. Clothing stores would have clothing, and perhaps shoes and other accessories. An example of a specialty shop might be one that sells antiques and vintage furniture. This business may also offer services, such as appraisal of furniture items, repairs, and a database of people from around the country who are looking for furniture, toys, and other collectibles.

The point I am making here is that you cannot be in business without having something to sell. This meets the definition of a business that makes it what is referred to as a "going concern."

"Going concern" is an accounting term for a company that has the resources needed to continue operating indefinitely until it provides evidence to the contrary. This term also refers to a company's ability to make enough money to stay afloat or to avoid bankruptcy.

The presumption of a going concern for the business also implies the basic declaration of intention to keep operating its activities at least for the next fiscal year, which is a basic assumption for preparing financial statements.

Deciding What to Sell as a Speaker

The most logical item for most speakers to sell is their book. Whether you have published a book or not, I want you to think much bigger and further out of the box as to what you will offer for sale.

First of all, selling from the stage or virtually, immediately after you have given a presentation is only one way to sell. Ellen and I both recommend you engage in online marketing, as we have done for many years. This entails setting up a simple blog and website where you will share your message with the world and offer visitors a way to sign up for your email list.

Once someone has joined your list, your goal is to communicate with them in a way that allows both you and your prospect to engage in a dialogue of sorts, where you send out email messages with some regularity and they are encouraged to respond back to you with their questions and comments. You will also make offers to your list that are relevant and appropriate for your topic.

Ellen and I also both use a "funnel" approach to selling our products and services. People who do not know you at all will initially arrive at one of your sites, or product pages, or your book's listing as visitors. Hopefully, they like what they see and resonate with your message enough to self-select as your prospect. This entails opting in to your list, following your author page on Amazon, or simply "liking" or retweeting your post on social media.

Because all of us are drawn to others who have a clear message, we resonate with I am comfortable with prospects taking their time to connect with me after they have found me. This requires a level of trust in the process where we must believe that our message and our marketing are strong enough to attract the right people into our community.

This funnel approach offers people a free gift of some type in exchange for their name and email address. Ellen has shared with you on this topic at length in Chapter 8, *The Art and Science of the Funnel*, so I will not reiterate any of the points she made. Instead, I want you to shift your thinking in this area so that you will see that selling something to someone who will benefit from it is a gift and a service to them.

Practice making an offer every time you interact with another person. This can be face to face or virtually. Turn it into a game and have fun with it. For example, when you are talking with a friend make it a point to recommend something to them.

I did this recently when a friend and I were discussing my ongoing Achilles tendon issue. Before she could ask me how I was doing with this, I shared that I no longer had the issue. I told her how a nutritionist had recommended I take collagen peptides every day. I purchased the powder at Amazon and had been adding it to my juice each morning. Within six weeks the problem was completely gone and even the doctor was baffled. Now I won't ever be without it and I gave her my affiliate link to the product. A side benefit of taking this is that collagen is thought of as being beneficial for your skin before joints and tendons, so you will end up with a smooth complexion as well.

Ask yourself what's for sale every time you interact with others. I blog regularly and include a call to action at the end of every post. This not only increases my income every day but also provides a valuable resource to my readers.

CHAPTER FIFTEEN

Selling from the Stage

"Great salespeople are relationship builders who provide value and help their customers win."
~ Jeffrey Gitomer

The first time someone explained to me what it meant to "sell from the stage" was in the summer of 2004, two years before I came to the realization that I needed to reinvent my life. This led to my making the conscious decision to resign from my job as a classroom teacher and to give away my best real estate clients to others who could better serve them.

On that day, I was sitting in the office of a man I continue to work with so he may help me with the financing of commercial properties I purchase as investments. We first talked about an apartment building I was planning to refinance because the interest rates had come down. We then switched to topics around what each of us was involved with away from real estate.

Geoffrey was telling me about a class he was taking, where he was learning how to speak on his topic of real estate investing and then sell a program at the end so that the attendees could continue to work him in the future. He said that he would speak and then sell from the stage in an attempt to have as many people as possible sign up for his offer.

He went on to share more details of what he intended to do, but I honestly had no experience in this area at that time. While he was talking, I thought back to the live presentations I had attended during the previous several years and I couldn't think of even one instance where someone had given a talk and then presented the audience with an offer to purchase something, whether it was real estate or something else.

Within a year that had all changed. In my quest to reinvent myself and create a different life I was invited to a spiritual event at a church in Los Angeles called Agape. The Reverend Michael Beckwith was speaking about the physics of prayer and meditation and I sat very still and listened intently to his message. At the end he offered us a set of CDs and a workbook so we could continue our study at home. On that day it was on sale for less than twenty dollars.

I turned to the friends who had invited me and they were smiling and nodding. They went to the small table in the back of the room and made their purchase, while I stayed in my seat and thought about this. I had decided not to buy anything on that day and I was sticking with my decision.

On the way out of the building they guided me into the bookstore. There, I made two purchases; one was a book they recommended to me and the other was an attractively designed bookmark with the name *Agape* etched in gold.

When I returned home later that day I thought about the events of the day and what had transpired. I had enjoyed the Reverend Beckwith's presentation. My purchase in the bookstore made sense to me. But the notion of having a speaker sell something to me and to the others in attendance at the end of their talk was a foreign one to me at that time. Then I put those thoughts out of my mind and began to read my new book.

Fast forward a few years and the notion of selling my products, courses, and programs from virtual and live stages has become my reality.

Once you have been introduced, taken the stage, looked your audience in the eyes, given everything you have during your presentation, and asked them to spend their money on what you have for sale, you will have mastered the art of selling from the stage. This skill is a valuable one that can change your life if you take it seriously and apply to your business.

Then your real work begins as you serve your customers so they will feel like they have made the best decision ever when they purchased and are on their way to becoming your raving fans. I have reframed my thinking around selling to include the concept of sharing valuable resources to those who are likely to benefit from them.

My Speaking Journey

My own journey to becoming a speaker was a fortuitous one, but once I felt the surge of energy that came from speaking in front of a group, I was ready to make it my mission to succeed in this arena.

It was a required class on public speaking in the 8th grade that initially introduced me to what it meant to speak in front of a group. Friends who had taken it first semester warned me of what lay ahead. Ten speeches of ten minutes each were assigned, with the topic announced one week in advance.

I dreaded this class. Even though I followed the instructions as to the outline, it was the delivery that was worse than death each week. The more I practiced, in front of my bedroom mirror and with my mother as a single audience member the less confident I became when it was my turn to present in front of the class. I wasn't alone in how I felt, but that did not make me feel any better.

The final assignment was to teach the class how to make or do something and I immediately thought of the egg carton Christmas ornaments we made at my house each year. I brought enough for everyone and set out the markers, glue, and glitter as I began to speak. This was fun! Even the boys showed interest in this project and I received a round of applause at the end.

What was different? Why did I enjoy preparing and delivering this speech so much? I believe it was because all eyes were not focused on me during my presentation and I could relax and share my knowledge and experience with the audience. That was my first stage, though I did not know that at the time. I sincerely believe that everything we do in life is preparing us for something we will do in the future. This applies across the board to our life experiences and was definitely the case with my career as a public speaker.

I successfully dodged public speaking for the next decade, until I received word that a childhood friend had died in a car accident and his mother asked me to say a few words at the funeral. Choking back my tears I was able to read a short note I had written about his life and what his friendship had meant to me over the years. My goal on that day was to let his family know what a treasured person he had been in my life and in the lives of others. There wasn't a dry eye in the house and I gave his mother a copy of what I had written in a card I had prepared for her the evening before.

I seldom gave a thought to speaking during my twenties. Public speakers were other people who were experts and authors and had skills I would never possess. As long as I told myself this it was the truth. When I became a classroom teacher at age thirty, I was asked to speak to the teachers at a staff meeting and all of the fear and insecurity I had experienced in my junior high speech class came flooding back. I was terrified and could feel the judgmental eyes of the other teachers piercing my psyche. I had to take their attention away from me so I asked them to count off from one to four as we went around the room. This gave me a minute to gather my thoughts but my presentation was weak and ineffective.

Once again, I withdrew from the idea of being a speaker and life continued to move forward. Twenty years later I made the conscious decision to leave teaching and my real estate business behind and start an online business I could run from home. Finally identifying as an introvert, I could replace my previous income while sitting in front of my computer by myself each day. I slowly grew my list and my income and loved this new lifestyle I was designing for myself.

Then a mentor suggested I begin speaking at marketing events. He suggested I attend a local Toastmasters meeting to get started. Earlier I wrote about the alliance that Toastmasters has recently formed with Rotary International that will benefit people all over the world.

Reluctantly I agreed to attend the meeting and thought maybe public speaking would be different all these years later. It wasn't. The Toastmasters group made a list of every little mistake you made and handed you the form when you were done. After going to a few more meetings, I decided I wanted to go a different direction if I were to become serious about speaking in public.

Soon after a woman I knew online asked me to speak at her marketing event in Raleigh, North Carolina. By this time, I was starting to attend live events around the U.S. and she knew I was having success in a variety of areas with my business. I made excuses as to why I would be unable to attend. She did her best to get me to change my mind but to no avail; I was too afraid to speak in front of a group of my peers and declined her invitation.

At this juncture I took a step back to think about my life and where I was going. Several people had already told me that public speaking would open doors for me. I was ready to shift my mindset around this precept and to do whatever was necessary to make it happen. Even if I didn't believe I had anything of value to say, I needed to speak to let others decide if what I would share with them could be of value.

I had joined my local Rotary Club and they were more than anxious to thrust a microphone into my hands each week. It started by the president asking me to tell the group about an upcoming project. My face would get red and my ears were hot as I mumbled into the microphone. I looked down at my feet and got my words out as quickly as possible before handing off the microphone to the next person. My heart would beat out of my chest and I couldn't hear anything for the next couple of minutes. It didn't seem to get any easier over time, but I continued to share information with the group. I later found out the others did not realize how nervous I was; most of what I was experiencing was all in my head.

One day the program chair asked me to give a talk about social media the following week. Before I could think of an excuse, I said that I would be happy to do this. I showed up early the next Wednesday, laptop in hand and ready to discuss Facebook and Twitter and how these social media platforms could be used for small business marketing.

It was fun! Just like when I was teaching 8th graders how to make Christmas decorations out of egg cartons almost four decades earlier, I loved showing my screen and answering questions from the group.

Within months I hosted a local event for about twenty-five small business owners where I shared how they could build a list and use email marketing to increase their business revenue. Social media was a part of what I taught on that day, as well as blogging for business. At the end of this four-hour long event, I had three new clients and lots of newly discovered self-confidence.

Soon, legendary marketer Matt Bacak called to invite me to speak at his event in Atlanta. I said yes before thinking and was excited at the prospect of speaking in this way. Matt was already something of a marketing legend and was barely thirty years old at the time. When his assistant emailed to ask for my PowerPoint slides, I answered that I was not going to use slides when I spoke at this event. Matt called me personally to say that I had to have slides and I agreed to put together a presentation he could take a look at.

I had taught PowerPoint to my 5th and 6th graders as a vocational skill in my classroom. I hadn't used that program since, but I dusted it off and created my first slides. I decided that sound and visual effects would not be suitable and came up with a presentation that covered all of my talking points and included an offer at the end.

There were several other speakers at Matt's event, including copywriter Ray Edwards and my very first mentor, Raymond Aaron. There was a man talking about investments, but he was so polished he seemed like an actor and did not sell anything that weekend. I made two sales of my twenty-five hundred dollar training program and was thrilled with my results. By the way, my presentation was awful and I even forgot to change out of my sneakers and into my good shoes before taking the stage. But I had accomplished my goal of speaking in front of an audience of more than five hundred people and selling from the stage.

Afterward I had lunch with Raymond Aaron. Actually, he ate and talked simultaneously and I took copious notes as to how I could improve my speaking the next time. Yes, there would be many "next times" in my future as a public speaker. Even Raymond invited me to speak at his events in Toronto and also in London within the next couple of years.

My new goal was to get in as much practice as possible between speaking at live events. Teleseminars and webinars were taking off as a way to communicate with your audience. YouTube made it simple to record a video on your smart phone and upload it to your channel. I visited as many Rotary Clubs as possible as a speaker, and soon I was invited to speak at the

District level to hundreds of people at a time. I was still nervous but speaking was becoming a much more positive experience for me.

Earlier I shared the story of how I came to speak at a marketing event hosted by my mentor, Armand Morin. I feel it is worthy of being shared again here.

When Armand asked me to speak at his upcoming event I hesitated before answering. Yes, I would speak. Thank you for this opportunity, I could hear myself saying. Back at home I worked on a new presentation and offer.

Before I went on stage in Minneapolis Armand saw me in the hallway and asked if I was nervous. I said,

"Armand, I'm nervous because I'm not nervous this time."

He laughed and threw up his hands in the air.

When I was introduced, I came out on stage and recognized that feeling in my stomach that let me know I would be nervous, at least for the first few minutes. Then something magical happened. I said something funny and someone in the audience laughed. Then I relaxed into my presentation and had even more interaction with the audience. I looked out at the sea of faces, most of whom did not know me at all. They were attentively watching and listening and I was having fun with them. I said a silent prayer of thanks and told myself to remember this moment forever. This was what I had always wanted and now it was happening for me.

That moment occurred over a decade ago and I can remember it as though it were yesterday. Everybody speaks every day and people want to hear from us. Now I speak all over the world to audiences of various sizes and on several topics, from how to write an eBook to changing your mindset to achieve greater success. I hope you take away something of value from what I have shared with you here and that you start speaking to share your thoughts, ideas, beliefs, experiences, and knowledge to people who can only hear your message from you.

Micro-Commitments

Have you ever heard the term "micro-commitment"? It's a valuable concept to familiarize yourself with, in my opinion and experience.

We use it a lot when measuring conversions and marketing strategies. You see every click and action taken by a new lead, a prospect, a reader and even a buyer is a micro-commitment. And when you've been able to turn a lead into a buyer that becomes a fully-fledged commitment. The buyer has made a commitment to you by giving you their payment. Now it's your job to ensure you hold up your end of the commitment.

The most excellent example I have seen of someone speaking at a live event and then selling from the stage was from the late Sylvie Fortin. In the spring of 2009 I was in Orlando, Florida to present at a marketing event hosted by my friend and mentor Armand Morin. Sylvie was the first speaker to come onstage and her presentation was about how and why the Amish are so successful in business. Sylvie was an incredible speaker and this was the best talk she ever gave, in my opinion, and her presentation has stayed with me over the years.

She began by showing a slide of a barn raising in the Amish community outside of Lancaster, Pennsylvania. You may have heard about the barn raisings the Amish are known for. This is a collective action of the community in which a barn for one of the members is built with the hands of the entire community. Instead of hiring outside workers or spending days or weeks doing it alone or with a few family members, the barn is raised within two days by all able-bodied people in the community. In modern times they now use a crane and a small crew, but the concept remains the same. Even though Sylvie chose to show us a slide instead of a video, we could see the strength and cooperation within the group in the photo.

Then Sylvie took two steps forward to be closer to the audience, leaned in as though she was about to share a secret with each of us individually and asked,

"Can you see how they are working together to accomplish their common goal?"

Yes, I could. I nodded and clapped along with the several hundred people in attendance on that day. What she was doing was asking us to commit so that we would be more engaged in her presentation.

I refer to this an "enrolling" the audience. When Ellen and I discussed this part of the book, she introduced me to a term called "micro-commitments" that is about drawing your audience in at every stage of your presentation and sales process.

As Sylvie moved further away from us upstage and continued, I was taken back to the days when I had walked in the midst of the Amish community and observed first-hand how they interacted with outsiders while I was visiting that part of Pennsylvania in 1979. Perhaps my mind wandered during this part of her presentation but it was well worth the result; she had transported me to another time and place and when my mind snapped back to the present time I was more deeply engaged than I had been at the very beginning.

She continued to enroll her audience at every turn by asking for these micro-commitments. Then she returned to her story of how the Amish worked together seamlessly to achieve common goals. Again, my mind wandered and I recalled my extended family in Finland talking about *talkoot*, a Finnish expression for a gathering of friends and neighbors organized to accomplish a task. This is similar to how the Amish accomplish bigger tasks in a short amount of time. This work is voluntary and unpaid.

Then I was pulled back abruptly into Sylvie's story. She laid out in detail how the Amish stick with the fundamentals of business. Instead of chasing after every shiny object that presents itself, they stick with what has worked for decades or longer. Business success using the Amish model relies on taking advantage of what you already have at your disposal to accomplish your goals.

This gentle, yet fast moving roller coaster of emotions took me over the edge and then back again several times during her presentation, leaving me feeling like I had climbed to the top of a mountain and accomplished a previously unfinished goal. It was exhilarating and satisfying and left me yearning for more. Sylvie closed most of the room into the reasonably priced program she was selling at the end. She had us early on and no one in the audience that day was expecting this result.

CHAPTER SIXTEEN

Speaking Online

"You can't convince anyone of anything. You can only give them the right information, so that they convince themselves."
~ Eben Pagan

I started speaking online in 2007 when a webinar company asked me to do a webinar on PowerPoint for their clients. They paid me a flat fee of $500 and they did the marketing for the webinar. I still remember how odd it was to be speaking to my computer instead of to real people but apparently it went well, because they ended up asking me back many times over the next two years.

Around 2009, I started doing my own webinars. Because I had developed a strong list of subscribers, I immediately had an audience. In 2010, I organized the Outstanding Presentations Workshop, an online summit with 6 – 7 speakers, including me. This catapulted me to the status of an expert on presenting because I was one speaker among many experts.

Since then, I have spoken online in many situations. I've continued to organize the Outstanding Presentations Workshop each year, spoken for third party organizations (sometimes reaching up to 3000 people), done sales webinars with affiliates, offered online training, and courses, spoken as a guest on podcasts, and more.

To give you an idea of the reach you can attain with online speaking, in the second year of the Outstanding Presentations Workshop, we got 3000 registrations from 97 countries. This worldwide reach was very inspiring for me. It's almost impossible to reach that many people from all around the world by speaking in front of a live audience.

Is there any downside to online speaking? The only one I can think of is that you have less rapport with your audience than when you are in front of a live audience.

On the plus side, you and your audience will save lots of time and money by not having to travel!

I am writing this during the Coronavirus pandemic, an event that has brought online speaking to the forefront. In fact, right now speaking online is the only way to speak to a group of people. The attack on 9/11 had a similar effect because people stopped traveling for a while and met online instead but I believe the coronavirus pandemic will have a longer-term effect on the way people speak.

This chapter includes information about speaking online in both selling and non-selling situations.

Opportunities Abound

One of the advantages of speaking online over speaking in front of a live audience is that it's MUCH easier to find places to speak. In fact, you can find boundless opportunities to speak. If you have an in-demand topic, are an engaging speaker, and let people know you want to speak, they will come to you.

But don't let that stop you from seeking out the best opportunities from your side.

Have a Strategy

Whenever you speak, you should have a strategy, a goal. Do you want to grow your list or sell? If you want to grow your list, what is your plan for turning the new subscribers into customers? How will this event give you visibility and how will you capitalize on that?

Having a strategy will ensure that you both get the results you want and help you avoid speaking engagements that are a waste of your time.

Always remember that the purpose of speaking is to get people to your website.

In this section on speaking online, I'll cover:

- The transformative effect of speaking online
- Speaking on podcasts
- Speaking on other online venues
- Looking good on camera
- Managing online meeting and webinar features

The Transformative Effect of Speaking Online

Let me tell you how historic I think the ability to speak online is compared to speaking live.

Both speaking and writing are ways to communicate. In the earliest days of humanity, we know that the development of language was a powerful transformation because it enabled people to communicate to each other so much more clearly. Much later came the development of writing which allowed people to put their thoughts on paper, except that it wasn't paper at that time--it was stone or papyrus.

The next major transformation was probably the invention of the printing press by Gutenberg. The printing press made it possible for the mass production of books so that an author could reach many more people. But because most people couldn't afford to print their own books, they were dependent on publishers to get out their message.

Much more recently with the development of the Internet, blogging became a way for writers to be able to reach the world without an intermediary such as a publisher. This was a transformative advance in the development of communication. In the same vein, the ability to self-publish books, especially e-books, made it possible for authors to be able to reach the world without getting the approval of a publisher.

For speaking, the equivalent of blogging and self-publishing books is speaking online. This can include webinars, online training, podcasts etc. As the speaker, you no longer need to be invited by an event organizer to speak. You can invite people to attend your online talk whenever you want.

That ability to reach the world with your message whenever you want is huge.

Speaking on Podcasts

I want to focus on podcasts before going on to other types of online speaking because they are an especially good way to speak if you're just starting out and because the principles of speaking on podcasts apply to other types on online speaking as well.

Note: Podcasts were originally audio only, but many are now in video format. This is technically called a vidcast, but many hosts use the word "podcast" even if they are using video.

If you think it's hard to find places to speak online, think again. Podcasts have become hugely popular and many podcasts need guests for each episode. Podcast producers are constantly looking for new guests and you can be one of them. Of course, not every podcast will give you the same amount of exposure. Just as you need to carefully choose your opportunities for in-person speaking, you need to evaluate podcasts as well.

Many podcast producers who invite guests have a specific format, a certain number of questions that they ask each guest. They're willing to give you those questions in advance so it's easy for you to prepare. You might also be able to suggest some questions that you would like to be asked. While the podcast is being recorded, you can have your notes in front of you. But don't sound like you're reading — be sure to speak enthusiastically, not like a robot.

As a podcast guest, not only or you expected to be an expert in your field and record a lively discussion, but the producer will want you to promote the podcast when it's published. The producer will also promote the podcast which is where you get your exposure.

Moreover, in almost all situations the podcast producer will offer you the opportunity to mention the URL of a free report of yours that listeners can download. As a result, podcasts are a great way to grow your list of email subscribers.

How to get interviews on podcasts

Create a list of podcasts in your niche. Here are 3 ways to find podcasts:

Use Google. You'll put in [your topic + podcast] without the brackets. This simple search should generate dozens of potential podcasts.

Search the Apple Podcasts directory, which you can find at podcasts.apple.com/us/genre/podcasts/id26. The directory has a huge list of podcasts that cover a variety of industries. Choose the category that closely describes your niche. Or open your Apple Podcasts app and use the Search box.

Here are some additional places to look for podcasts:

- BlogTalkRadio.com
- Stitcher.com
- TuneIn.com
- Spreaker.com
- Interview Guests Directory, which you can find at interviewguestsdirectory.com
- Perfect Podcast Guest at perfectpodcastguest.com/
- Radio Guest List at radioguestlist.com
- PodcastGuest at podcastguests.com

You don't have to restrict your appearances to podcasts in your niche. You may want to be featured on podcasts that have crossover appeal for your audience. For example, if you teach people how to speak more effectively, as I do, you might want to appear on podcasts aimed at salespeople, trainers, and entrepreneurs — 3 very different niches — because they all need to speak more effectively.

When you create your list, filter the results by these factors:

- **Popularity and ratings:** If no one is watching or the podcast has low ratings, skip it
- **If it fits into your marketing:** The audience for the podcast should be your target market
- **If the host features interviews:** Some podcasts are presentations by the podcaster, so they don't take guests

Once you've found some podcasts that look like a good fit, it's time to start building a relationship. Here are some steps to follow:

1) Listen to 2-3 recent episodes
2) Subscribe to the host's newsletter
3) Follow the host on social media
4) Send a personal email (or perhaps Facebook/LinkedIn message) describing why you were attracted to the podcast and asking for a meeting to discuss if you could be a guest.
5) Provide some information about yourself. You want to mention your story and experience and how it relates to their audience. If you have a speaker one-sheet, include that as well.
6) Don't forget to include your contact details. Ideally, you want to add a website where the host can learn more about you and even see you speak. Some hosts have a form for you to fill out with the information they require.

Tip: If you know any of the previous guests, the BEST way to get an invitation to speak is to ask that guest to introduce you to the podcaster. This applies to many speaking opportunities.

Preparing to be a podcast guest

When you meet with the podcaster — or discuss your episode by email or message — be sure to get the following information:

- **Your topic:** You should have an exact name for your episode. This is usually an agreement between the two of you.
- **Length of appearance:** You should know how long you'll be speaking
- **Type of episode:** Is it an interview? Do you do a presentation? Most podcasts will be interviews.
- **Questions you'll be asked:** Many podcasters have a set series of questions they ask all their guests, such as "What book are you reading now?" or "How did you get into the field you're in?" Podcasters want you to be prepared, so they'll usually give you the questions in advance.
- **What you can offer:** In most cases, you can offer an opt-in gift, but check. In some cases, the podcaster will just want you to provide contact information. In a few cases, you can sell a product or service.
- **Publish date:** Podcasts are recorded in advance. You want to know when your episode will be published to you can plan to promote it and evaluate the results (subscriptions, for example).

Often, you'll get an immediate invitation to speak. Be careful to put your appointed time to record the podcast on your calendar. Then, you're ready to prepare.

The podcaster will have instructions for you about equipment, being in a quiet location, etc. Make sure you can fulfill the requirements. You'll need a good microphone or headset. Use earplugs if you don't use a headset (which is a combination of microphone and headphones) to avoid feedback between your mic and your computer speakers.

Sometimes you'll use Skype; if so, you need the Skype desktop app and an account.

Work on your content and be sure to practice, especially if you're new at this. If you'll be giving a presentation, you need to time it in advance to make sure it fits into the time you'll be given. If you'll be interviewed, write out the answers to the questions in advance so you won't hem and haw.

Create an opt-in gift on a landing page, if that's what you have agreed on. Have a special, short URL that your listeners can remember and easily type in, even on their phone.

Make sure that your opt-in gift will appeal to the podcast's target market. It should be something valuable and relevant to their needs.

During the podcast session

Make sure you won't be interrupted. I close the door to my office and put a sign on it that I'm recording. There was a funny incident on the BBC when Professor Robert Kelly's live television interview on the topic of Korea was interrupted by his two children. You can Google it.

Be careful not to make inadvertent noises. I was once told that I was hitting something — perhaps my desk — and I wasn't even aware of it! Your mic will pick up the slightest noises. Of course, you should turn off the sound on your phone – your mic will even pick up vibrations if you use the Vibration setting.

Give your full attention to your session. If you've written out answers to the questions, have them available, whether printed or on your screen. But be careful not to shuffle papers or click your mouse while you're speaking — yes, the mic will pick all of that up.

Following up after your podcast episode

As soon as the podcast is published, thank the podcaster and share it with your list and on social media. Spend a few days promoting the interview.

Tip: Reach out to the podcaster and ask if he or she needs another guest. If so, recommend someone else. The podcaster will greatly appreciate this and may refer you to more speaking opportunities or partner with you in another way. Definitely look into further partnership opportunities with the podcaster!

Continue to promote your podcast episode. Every time someone listens to the podcast, you might get a subscriber. One of the great things about podcasts is that they are around for a long time and can bring you a stream of subscribers on an ongoing basis.

Some podcasters will give you the MP3 file of the podcast and let you use it on your website, with a link to their podcast. With permission, you can even transcribe it and reuse it as a blog post, report or e-book. In other words, there are lots of ways to repurpose your podcast session to grow your list and bring in more income.

Other Online Speaking Opportunities

I started by going deep into podcasts, but they are really only a drop in a huge bucket of places to speak online. You can speak online on Facebook and YouTube, on video streaming services, on online meetings or webinars, and as a speaker on web summits.

Live streaming

Live streaming means that the video of you speaking is streamed over the Internet in real time. People can see and hear you as you talk. Often, they can comment as well. The effect is very interactive. A downside is that you can't edit your video—whatever happens, people see. Usually, however, you can download the recording and edit it afterward. Also, you can always delete the video if you want.

For example, you can speak online on Facebook using the Facebook Live feature. You can speak on your own timeline, in a group you own (or one that gives you permission), or on a page you own. I speak weekdays for 3-5 minutes in my private Facebook group for my membership program. This is like Toastmasters Table Topics – I decide on a topic and then speak extemporaneously. It's great speaking practice!

Then, in my public Change the World Marketing Facebook group, I do one longer Facebook Live at the same time each week. I prepare a topic in advance and write out a few notes. Twice, I've done hour-long Facebook Lives and I prepared a detailed script for each. Mostly, I speak for about 15 minutes.

A less common way of speaking online is to be a guest on a Facebook Live. This requires some additional software, such as Zoom, Ecamm (Mac only), BeLive, or Streamyard. Usually, the owner of the page or group will introduce and interview you.

There are lots of other places to live stream yourself speaking. Each platform has its advantages and disadvantages. Here are some of the most popular options:

- YouTube Live
- Vimeo

- Instagram Live (part of Instagram stories, viewable only on mobile devices)
- Google Meeting

Webinars

Webinars are another way to speak live while online. People hear you in real time, but a webinar is generally by invitation only. On the other hand, you can invite large numbers of people to attend.

Webinars require a webinar service. Examples are Zoom Webinar, GotoWebinar, WebEx, Google Hangouts, Adobe Connect, and Microsoft Teams.

You can use webinars to sell your product or service, for training existing customers, employees and team members, and to hold meetings. Examples of training for customers are online courses, membership or group coaching meetings, or offer Q&A sessions.

You might present on your own webinar service's account or be invited to speak on someone else's account.

Web summits are online conferences that may include many sessions. In many cases, each speaker promotes the web summit, which can result in large numbers of registered participants.

Some web summits allow you to sell and even encourage it. Others require you to stick to offering your free report.

How do you prepare for a webinar? You can have a script, but you still need to practice, because you shouldn't be reading word for word. If you're new at webinars, practice will also help you become accustomed to using the technology. It's common to use slides during a webinar.

Here are 7 mistakes to avoid when doing webinars:

Reading the slides: You've seen this a million times as a webinar attendee. The speaker shows slide after slide of bulleted text and mostly reads it with a few additions. Just as those speakers bored you if you do the same, you'll bore your audience. Instead put less text on each slide be sure to collaborate on the text that's on each slide and use a large relevant image

Staying on the same slide for more than two minutes: I'm being very generous. Actually, 2 minutes is a long time for your audience to watch the same slide when they can't see you. Yes, they can hear you, but vision trumps hearing -- that's just how the brain works. Use more slides than you would for a live presentation. I recommend changing slides every 30 to 60 seconds in most cases.

Using animation too much or too little: You might think, "Why not make the text fly in?" But animated text is annoying; Your audience will hate it. Moreover, the animation may be somewhat blurry over the webinar connection. On the other hand, a simple animation that actually makes the point clearer, such as an animated diagram showing a step-by-step process, can help keep your audience interested. The Appear animation will always look crisp as long as you don't use many animations too quickly one after the other.

Not using interactive features: Almost all web and or services have interactive features and you should use them as much as possible. Invite attendee contributions by asking them questions. Ask them to use the Chat feature. If the service doesn't let attendees see each other's comments, read them out loud just as you repeat a question in a live presentation so that everyone can hear. Use the Poll feature. I always try to engage the audience in some way within the first 5 minutes of the webinar and then several times throughout.

Talking in a monotone and hiding behind the slides: Because people can't see you unless you show your webcam, your voice needs to be more lively than usual. Standing as you speak as a helpful technique to make you sound more powerful. If you have a script -- and you should -- be careful not to sound as if you're reading it. You can accomplish this by practicing, recording your practice and listening to the recording. You'll know right away if you need to work on how your voice sounds. I recommend using the webcam. Just as seeing you isn't distracting when you present in front of a live audience, it isn't distracting during a webinar. However, if your Internet connection starts stuttering, turn off the webcam because that will reduce the bandwidth you need. (I recommend always using a wired Internet connection when on a webinar or livestreaming – it's more reliable than Wi-Fi.)

Not providing follow-up: Attendees are generally alone when they attend your webinar -- at home, in their office, at their desk. Their attention tends to wander because they can't see you or because they know that you can't see them. They need follow up to connect further with you and to cement their understanding of your content. Here are some techniques you can use:

- Offer a handout at the end of the web
- Send a follow up email asking for questions and comments with a link to further resources. In fact, you should send several follow-up emails
- Invite people to make an appointment with you

Once you do a few webinars, you'll see their power for growing your speaking career and business.

Looking Good on Camera

Of course, you want to look good on camera. The good news is you don't have to spend a lot of time or money. More importantly, don't obsess over how you look. You're probably more sensitive about your looks than necessary and your viewers don't care nearly as much as you do.

Here are 5 aspects to looking good on camera:

- You: hair, makeup, clothes
- Lighting
- Audio
- Background
- Video quality

Let's discuss each aspect separately.

You: This involves your hair, your makeup, and your clothes. Mainly, you want to look neat and professional, without spending a lot of time. Yes, this applies to both women and men.

When you practice, you can see how you'll look. Find a routine that gives you the best results in the least amount of time.

Lighting: Without good lighting, you can look like a ghost and people can't see your face. The easiest solution is to face a window so that daylight shines on your face. If you can't do that, experiment with various lighting until your face looks bright without too many shadows. You can buy a ring light to light up your face. Here's one that you can buy on Amazon: amzn.to/3eR53yo

Audio: You need a good microphone and a place without distracting background noises or too much echo. Turn off your phone. Also, be careful not to hit your computer with your watch or use your mouse (more than absolutely necessary) while you're speaking. You'll find several microphones at amazon.com/shop/influencer-efa2ffa2.

Background: Your background should not be distracting and should look neat and professional. A folding screen can be an easy solution. Some services let you create an artificial background with or without a green screen.

Video quality: Your webcam should record at high definition, at least 780p, so that the video doesn't look grainy. If the webcam on your laptop is old, invest in an add-on like the Logitech C920. You can check it out at amzn.to/2KAkH3t.

Here are some other tips for making a good impression:

- Use the webcam. As I mentioned earlier, some people "hide behind the slide" but you'll engage your audience more if they can see you
- Use your voice to keep your audience's attention – vary the pitch and speed and use pauses.
- Use your hands, just as you would in front of a live audience
- Stand up. Most speakers don't do this, but you'll have more energy and people will notice the difference. If you don't have a stand-up desk, you can put your computer on some boxes.
- Look at the camera. Try to get in the habit of looking at the webcam itself, not the image of yourself on your screen, which is lower.
- Practice, record and then watch for distracting motions like touching your hair or looking up as you think

Managing Online Meeting and Webinar Features

How often have you seen a webinar in which it was clear that the presenter didn't know the webinar software, didn't practice, and didn't have someone to provide backup support when things went wrong?

Learn the settings of the webinar software you're using

The more you know the interactive features of the software, the more engaging your webinar will be. When you know how to handle glitches and audience questions about the software, their experience will be smoother.

An assistant is helpful if there are technology glitches and for monitoring audience questions and comments.

Having a second monitor will help you display the chat without covering up your slides.

Especially if you're using the webcam, connect to the Internet via an Ethernet cable. It's more reliable than Wi-Fi in most cases.

As I'm writing this, people have started taking advantage of public webinars to maliciously interfere with the speaker. This has become known as "Zoombombing." Here are some tips on keeping your webinar safe in Zoom –if you're using another technology, you should find similar settings.

https://www.techrepublic.com/article/how-to-prevent-zoom-bombing-5-simple-tips/

PART IV

Using the Power of Stories in Your Speaking and Business

"Stories are 22 times more memorable than facts alone..."
~ Jennifer Aaker

As a speaker, you're probably well aware of the power of stories. But you may not have thought about how useful stories are for a business. As a matter of fact, stories are crucial for creating a brand, retaining loyal customers, and inspiring new customers.

Imagine a rapt audience listening to the story of how you overcame obstacles and succeeded beyond your wildest dreams. The effect of a well-crafted, relevant story is unlike any other content you write – it has a much more emotional effect.

The chapters in this part explain how you can use stories in your talks to grow your business.

CHAPTER SEVENTEEN

Stories Are More Memorable

"Once upon a time..."
~ From most fairy tales

You can explain a principle, but if you also tell a story about it, people are more likely to remember it. We forget facts and figures, we forget principles and tenets, but we remember stories.

Jennifer Aaker, Professor of Marketing at Stanford Graduate School of Business, says "Stories are 22 times more memorable than facts alone... Studies show that we are wired to remember stories much more than data, facts, and figures. However, when data and story are used together, audiences are moved both emotionally and intellectually."

All I Remember Is Two Stories...

I majored in History in college – not for any good reason except that I liked it. I studied Russian History, History of the American West, World War II, and much more.

That was many years ago and I recently realized how little I remembered. In fact, all I remember is two stories. One is the story of the Donner family in History of the American West. The Donner Party, or Donner–Reed Party, was a group of American pioneers that set out for California in a wagon train in May 1846. They were delayed by a series of mishaps and mistakes and spent the winter of 1846–47 snowbound in the Sierra Nevada mountains. I won't retell it here but you can look it up if you want. This story doesn't have a happy ending – it was shocking actually – as many of them didn't survive.

The other story was from my Russian History class. Tsar Peter the Great was 6 feet 8 inches tall. This was very unusual in those days. In 1697, he decided to travel "incognito" to Western

Europe for 18 months with a large delegation. He used a fake name to escape social and diplomatic events, but since he was so much taller than almost anyone else, he did not fool anyone of importance. So, everyone had to pretend that they didn't know who he was!

I remember our professor painting this picture for us and thinking how funny it was. I never forgot this story. Even 40 years later, I remember the basics of these two stories.

That's the power of stories.

The Value of Attention

These days, the attention of your audience is split. There are always interruptions demanding attention. Yet attention is what you need. If you can stand out from the crowd, people will remember you.

Stories help you get attention. It's our nature to pay attention to a good story. In a later chapter, we'll cover the parts of a good story.

The Importance of Emotion

You may have heard the idea that people buy on emotion and in fact, there's plenty of research showing this. Of course, people make decisions in different ways, but emotion is almost always important.

Stories are great at portraying emotion—they can be happy or sad, funny or serious, inspiring or boring. You can move people to feel the urgency and intensity of their problem more easily with a story than with facts. That doesn't mean that you shouldn't use facts, just that it's important to evoke emotion as well.

Harvard professor Gerald Zaltman wrote that 95% of purchasing decisions are unconscious and that most of the unconscious urges are related to emotion. He concludes that emotion is what really drives purchasing behaviors.

I sometimes tell the story of why my husband went out to buy two parakeets for our two sons and came back with four. They were on sale and he couldn't resist getting a good bargain. Yes, four parakeets still cost more than two and were more expensive (and time consuming) to take care of, but they were on sale!

We'll talk more about emotion in a later chapter.

Chapter Eighteen

Speaking to Inspire and Persuade

"Your customer should be the hero of the story, not your brand."
~ Donald Miller

As a speaker, you need to learn the skill of inspiring and persuading your audience. You can add inspirational and persuasive components to any talk, but obviously some talks will require more than others.

For example, if you're teaching a course, you aren't selling and might be conveying lots of details. Yet you still need to inspire your students to be excited about the results they will get so they will implement the steps you're teaching.

No matter the situation, you can inspire people.

Are sales up? Thanks those who contributed, talk about what the future will be like if it continues.

Are sales down? If you can, talk about how they can turn things around. Or mention, if it's true, that the trend is probably temporary. Or inspire people to take action, to make changes to turn things around.

Never forget that you have the power to uplift others. To move people to change themselves and to change the world.

If you are trying to turn your speaking into an online business, in most situations you'll be doing a lot of inspiration and persuasion.

Persuasion and inspiration are connected, but inspiration focuses on being uplifting and evoking positive emotion.

You're inspiring people to buy, to take action, even just to implement the training you're providing.

Both inspirational and persuasive presentations usually have a call to action. For a persuasive talk, the desired action might be a purchase or approval. For an inspirational talk, the desired action might be to donate money or time.

What Makes a Talk Inspiring?

An inspiring talk uplifts people so that they leave feeling positive, energized, and ready to take action. Even if you just want people to buy, adding inspirational elements will be effective.

But how do you get there?

The technique is to use a storytelling arc that has a beginning, middle, and end. And to focus on the place that the people in your audience have in that story.

Beginning Your Story Arc

There's a dream (Think of Martin Luther King Jr.'s "I have a dream.") Your dream might be a goal for a business or to help the homeless or to improve the lives of children.

You describe the current situation and then inspire people with the dream. What is the NOW? Why is change necessary?

Here you define the problem. It could be poor sales results or homelessness or high blood pressure.

You talk about the journey ahead, what needs to be done.

Let's look at part of the Gettysburg Address from President Abraham Lincoln. (In fact, this is the end of that very short talk and repeating what needs to be done at the end works very well.)

"It is rather for us to be here dedicated to the great task remaining before us—that from these honored dead we take increased devotion to that cause for which they gave the last full measure of devotion—that we here highly resolve that these dead shall not have died in vain—that this nation, under God, shall have a new birth of freedom—and that government of the people, by the people, for the people, shall not perish from the earth."

In a workshop for non-profits that I conducted on inspirational presentations, one of the attendees chose a dream of more people adopting dogs from shelters instead of buying them.

What do YOU want to change? What's YOUR dream?

What does your audience want to change? What's THEIR dream?

Creating the Middle of Your Story Arc

There are obstacles to overcome. People need to be inspired to climb over them. This often involves teamwork.

So, in the middle of your talk, with people inspired by the goal, you tell them about what needs to be done, including the obstacles they need to remove.

You lay out the path to the solution. What steps are necessary to bring about desired change?

What are the obstacles? If there weren't obstacles, you probably wouldn't need to give your speech. If you don't acknowledge the obstacles, people will get disillusioned during the process of change.

In some cases, you will provide details and procedures. In other situations, your audience members will be responsible for figuring out how to get to the goal.

Tell your audience that they have the knowledge and skills to get past anything. Perhaps that's just what you're there to give them. Or you might support them along the way.

For example, if you're selling software, there might be a learning curve that could be an obstacle. Then you'll tell them about your Support Desk and how quickly you respond to questions.

Ending Your Story Arc

The end is the most important because you want people to go away optimistic and uplifted. Help them imagine life when the goal is obtained. This is the vision you dreamed about.

People arrive at the goal, hopefully. They get the promised reward. They're congratulated. There's a group feeling of accomplishment. You describe how it feels, what it looks like, and the benefits.

Where Is Your Audience Now?

Now, it depends where your audience in the story. Maybe you're trying to get people to change, you're at the beginning. Maybe they're in the middle and you're trying to get them to persevere. Maybe you're at the end and either celebrating or trying to inspire them to start over.

In your talk, you'll emphasize the next step. Recap what has already happened, and then focus on the next part of the story.

Putting Your Story Arc Together

To put your story arc together, answer these questions:

[Beginning] Let's dream! What would you like to change?

[Beginning] What is the NOW? Why is change necessary?

[Middle] What steps do you think are necessary for the desired change to come about?

[Middle] What are the obstacles?

[Middle] What are some ways to overcome the obstacles?

[End] Imagine life when the goal is obtained.

You might have noticed that there is some repetition. For example, you'll talk about the goal both at the beginning and at the end. That's OK. Envisioning the goal is the most inspiring part!

The Power of Images

Besides using words, you can increase the inspirational power of your talk with images. Images help you evoke emotions, which are an integral part of inspiration and persuasion.

You can use images on slides or simply use image-rich language. Here's a brief example from Martin Luther King's "I Have a Dream" speech:

"Now is the time to rise from the dark and desolate valley of segregation to the sunlit path of racial justice. Now is the time to lift our nation from the quicksands of racial injustice to the solid rock of brotherhood."

Can you see how he uses image-rich language and contrasts the beginning (now) and end states?

If you're using slides, be sure not to make them a wall of text. These slides distract your audience from you. Instead, use large, striking images and make people listen to you to understand their meaning.

A helpful technique is to point only one point on a slide and match a simple statement with an evocative image.

In the next chapter, I'll talk about using stories because they are another way to inspire and persuade your audience.

CHAPTER NINETEEN

The Six Kinds of Stories You Can Tell

"Tell me and I forget; teach me and I may remember; involve me and I learn."
~ Xun Kuang

What types of stories can you tell for your business? Here, we're distinguishing between stories in your talks and stories that you use to persuade people to subscribe or buy a product. The stories in your talks will be about the content and may not be designed to be persuasive yet they'll still help your readers to remember your content better.

There are six types of stories you can tell; we explain them in the next few paragraphs.

Your Company/Brand Story

This is one of the most important stories you can tell. It's the origin story of your company or brand. Why did you start it? What problems do you solve for customers? What do you stand for? What have you accomplished? How did it happen?

This story will help you potential customers decide if they want to do business with you.

An example is the story of TOMS, which sells shoes as well as other products.

While traveling in Argentina in 2006, TOMS Founder Blake Mycoskie witnessed the hardships faced by children growing up without shoes. Wanting to help, he created TOMS Shoes, a company that would match every pair of shoes purchased with a new pair of shoes for a child in need. One for One®.

The Personal Story

A personal story is a story from someone's life, usually yours. It could be how you overcame difficulties to reach the place where you are today.

Many personal stories involve overcoming difficulties. They help your potential customers feel that they can overcome their difficulties as well.

Here is one of the personal stories I tell...

Years ago, I wrote a quarterly article for the magazine Presentations – which is no longer published. In January, 2004, I wrote an article called "Presentations Without Bullets."

I created a screenshot of a slide for the article that was so ugly that a reader wrote a letter to the editor asking, "How could you publish such a bad example of a slide? It has no focus. Please, give us better examples!" And they published that letter in the magazine the following month.

As you can imagine, I was mortified, embarrassed beyond belief when I read it. So, I decided that I would learn how to design slides. I wasn't a designer, so I had to start from scratch.

I started going to a PowerPoint conference every year. I read books and I read research on what types of presentations work best. Over the years and many presentations, I figured out the techniques that I could use to help my clients succeed with their own presentations.

As a result of all my studying, in 2010, I became PowerPoint MVP (Most Valuable Professional). MVP is a Microsoft award, the highest award that Microsoft gives to experts in its products. MVPs have to contribute at no charge to the user community, which I do with the free content on my blog, by giving free webinars, and more. I have to reach a lot of people, which I do – my EllenFinkelstein.com website reaches about 100,000 people each month and my PowerPoint Tips newsletter goes out to about 12,000 people.

The combination of what I learned and the MVP award helped me create a thriving business.

The value of this story is that it helps potential customers realize that if I could learn to design slides without any artistic talent, they can, too.

The Product Story

You can tell stories that relate to products. Your story could be how the product was developed, why it came into existence, a problem the product makers had to solve, or how a customer used it in a creative way. If you have one product, this might be the same as the company/brand story.

A good example of a product story is the one about the origin of the idea for the Sony Walkman. Masaru Ibuka, Sony's co-founder, often travelled for business and he liked to listen to music. However, he hated dragging around a bulky cassette player. He asked his engineers to create something smaller and more portable – just for playback and for use only with headphones – and the Walkman was born. This gave us not only the Walkman, but, by extension, all of the portable music players we use today.

The Customer Story

Tell how your customers relate to your product or service. This is a great story because it emphasizes the benefits of what you offer. When people read about a customer's experience with your product or service, they put themselves in the customer's shoes and see how your products or services can benefit them.

This type of story can be similar to a case study but it's more general.

The Employee Story

Employee stories are engaging because they take your readers and viewers behind the scenes and add a human element to your company. These stories help to convey your corporate culture.

An employee story might tell how an employee improved a product or service, helped the company reach one of its goals, or bent over backwards for a customer in need.

The Case Study

A case study is a more detailed and researched story of an event in your company. The most typical one is the story of how you helped a customer improve results. For example, maybe you helped a customer increase sales by 20%.

A case study includes specific data that you can verify. A case study might be a detailed retelling of a customer or employee story.

Chapter Twenty

How to Make Stories Relevant

"Staying relevant requires learning."
~ Mark Cuban

Stories must be relevant to your audience and readers if they are to be effective. They need to have a purpose. Another way to say this is that you need to use stories strategically, with a goal in mind.

Knowing Your Audience

The first step to making your stories relevant is knowing your audience. What do they think their problem is? What will help them solve their problem? What are their limiting beliefs that stop them from solving their problem? What objections will they come up with to stop them from buying or subscribing? What are their values and what emotions speak the most to them?

You may need to do some market research to gather your audience's demographics, such as age, economic level, location, gender and so on, as well as their psychographics. Psychographics are thoughts, feelings, opinions, values and attitudes. Some marketers pay too much attention to demographics and too little to psychographics. Attitudes and values play a very important part in storytelling. If your story is in tune with your audience, it will resonate with them.

Deciding on Your Most Effective Message

Based on your audience and your strategic goals, what is your best message? What message will draw your audience to you? What is it that you really want to say?

Your story is a way of expressing that message, a metaphor that makes your point in a more engaging and personal way.

Let's say that many of my readers want a successful online business but don't take the necessary action because of doubts or fears.

And let's say that I want my message to be that you have to learn to take decisive action if you want to succeed in your own business.

Now that I have decided on my audience and the message I want to convey, I'm ready to build my story.

Chapter Twenty-One

The 4 Cs of Story Structure

"The key to a good story structure is to write a great beginning and a great ending and keep them close together."
~ Anonymous

Once you've decided on the type of story you want to tell and the message you want to give them, you are ready to write it. You can use the "4 C's" to make sure you include all the necessary elements and structure. Including the 4 C's in each story will help ensure that you have the desired effect.

Here are the 4 C's and how to use them:

1. Context

   The context sets not only the location of the story but the situation the characters find themselves in. Provide some visual detail about the situation. It establishes the relevance of the story to the audience (see more about this in the next chapter).

   Use the Context section to create a "hook" that captures the attention of your readers or audience. What is unusual about the situation? Think about how to create anticipation to hear the rest of the story.

2. Characters

   After you set the context, you need to say something about the characters, the people in the story. They should relate to your audience in some way.

   The characters have a problem or are in a situation that needs resolution. Your audience will identify with one or more of the characters in the story.

   Bring your characters alive by quoting them directly or describing how they look.

3. Conflict
   Focus on the conflict which is the heart of your story. The conflict or obstacle can be of ideas against ideas or people against people. It could be an internal conflict. Give some intensity to the conflict or obstacle that your audience can identify with.
4. Conclusion
   In your conclusion, describe how the obstacle was overcome or the conflict resolved. Usually, you want your story to have a happy ending, although not always. (A story of failure can also help your audience understand what they need to do.)
   Remember your message? Don't assume that your audience will "get it." State the "moral" of the story clearly.

CHAPTER TWENTY-TWO

Engaging Your Audience

> *"I've learned that people will forget what you said, people will forget what you did, but people will never forget how you made them feel."*
> *~ Maya Angelou*

We've talked about the types of stories you can tell, how to make them relevant, and how to structure them, but storytelling is an art, too. In this chapter, we'll explain some of the finer details of storytelling that will make your stories more powerful.

Create an Emotional Connection

As we've noted, a good story makes an emotional connection. Why do non-profits focus on one hungry child rather than the statistics of how many hungry children there are? Because you can't feel compassion about numbers, but you can about that one child.

Why do security companies create ads about thieves – online and in your home? That fear convinces buyers to buy security hardware and software.

Why do business coaches talk about their lifestyle? Because the desire for that lifestyle pushes people to buy their coaching.

When your story is genuine and from the heart and touches on your readers' pain, it will be persuasive. When you meet them where they are and clearly describe where they want to go, you'll get results.

When your readers can relate to the characters in your story, it keeps them riveted. They're rooting for the hero and hoping that she'll succeed. They identify with the hero, which may just be you, if you're telling your personal or company story. They want to be a hero, too.

Create Suspense and Anticipation

Suspense and anticipation are important in any story. They keep the audience glued to the story to see what will happen in the end. Although everybody knows that the children in the plastic bubble gyrosphere in "Jurassic World" won't get eaten by the dinosaur that's chomping on the bubble, we're glued to the screen to see what will happen.

How can you add suspense to your story? By emphasizing the risks you took or how you felt during crisis. How close to failing did you come? Although your readers know that you came out all right, they'll follow along with you if you explain the fear you felt or the doubt you experienced. They may be feeling the same fear and doubt and will be carried along with you.

Inspire People to Action

Stories don't have to be inspirational to be interesting – some famous stories are tragedies, after all – but for stories in a marketing context, you want to inspire your audience. Remember that hungry child? The fundraising ad isn't supposed to drive you to despair and give up hope. The conclusion is always, "You can make a difference."

Inspiration is important in marketing because it persuades people to take action. Taking action could mean buying a product, subscribing to your free offer, or sharing a blog post you wrote. Stories without hope and inspiration don't lead the audience to take action.

So, after telling an inspirational story of some success you had, you can say, "If I could do this, so can you, IF you take the next step." In business, every story should have a call to action.

Let Your Personality Come Through

In whatever story you tell, your personality should play a major part. This is why marketers so often start sales webinars with some background about their personal life. Think about how your past led you to your current business and why. Then tell that story.

I told you the story of how I learned how to design slides (and teach others to design them). It started with someone complaining about how bad a slide of mine was and that spurred me to learn simple and effective methods of design. I then turned that into a method (the Tell 'n' Show℠ method) that anyone can apply.

Keep People Attentive

One effective storytelling technique is to break up the story. Instead of telling the entire story all at once, offer just the first part. This is a good way to keep your audience paying attention to hear the rest. It's like a weekly TV serial that ends on a cliffhanger. You'll come back to watch the next week to see what happens.

You might break up your story only for a few minutes in a video. On a sales page, you can start a story at the top and tell them you'll tell them more in a minute, which is really at the bottom of the page.

This technique is called creating a loop. You open the loop but don't close it right away, keeping your audience rapt because they want to hear the ending.

Create Viral Stories

Content that gets widely shared or goes viral online has one thing in common – it elicits strong emotions. These stories could be awe-inspiring, funny, moving, illuminating, inspiring, shocking, sexy, scary, infuriating or controversial. Spicing your stories up with these emotions will help your stories get liked, shared, and linked to, but make sure they're right for your brand and audience. As they say, it's always wise to avoid politics and religion!

Make Stories Visual

The more visual elements you can add into your story, the more likely your audience will tell their friends and colleagues about it. If you're speaking without presentation slides, use words to describe the scene. How did it look, smell, sound, taste, and feel?

If you can incorporate pictures and video, that's even more powerful. In fact, you can create images that tell stories without any words at all. The reason visual elements make stories more effective is that they more directly trigger emotions.

Photographs and live videos will usually do this more effectively than illustrations and cartoons because they're more realistic. A photo of a hungry child is way more touching than a drawing of one.

CHAPTER TWENTY-THREE

Choose the Best Media for Your Story

"Photography is a way of feeling, of touching, of loving. Images remember little things, long after you may have forgotten everything. And a particularly moving image can teach empathy."
~ Dorothea Lange

In the last chapter, we started talking about images and video and in this chapter, we'll go a little more deeply into media because you can tell a story through any type of media, whether it's text, images, or video.

Your Story Extends Beyond Your Talk

When you think about moving from a talk to a thriving business, you need to understand that your story will go beyond your talk. People may tell others about the stories in your book because people love to retell stories.

You may use short versions of a story in a group coaching session, on a Facebook Live, or on a webinar. And we'll talk in a minute about using stories when speaking to a live audience – very important!

The more fundamental the lesson of your story, the more it will spread and the more places you'll be able to use it. Children's stories are good examples of this. When my children wouldn't help in the kitchen, I told them the story of The Little Red Hen. (If you don't know that story, look it up.)

Use Text to Tell a Story

Many stories are told in text. As a speaker, you may not think about turning your story into text. You can use it if your write a book, on your website's About page, in a free offer, in social media posts, etc.

When writing your story for your talks, don't try to sound formal or overly literate. Write using an informal, personal tone that's easy for your audience to understand and relate to.

Finally, speak out the story and make sure it is relevant and provides value to your readers. Will they learn something useful and they can put into action?

I recommend recording yourself telling the story (I recommend this for your entire talk) and listening back to it to get a more objective perspective.

Use Video to Tell a Story

I just explained that you can record your story for practice purposes, but of course, you can keep the recording and use it as a video on your website, in an online course platform, on sales pages, on your About page, on your Home page, on video platforms (YouTube, Vimeo, etc.) and on social media.

Just a few years ago, creating a video was difficult and expensive. Now, it's as easy as taking out your smartphone or using your computer's webcam.

Here are some tips for turning your story into a video—many of these apply to recording your entire talk:

Make it Short and Simple

For a story, just keep it short.

On YouTube, videos need to be especially short. Research has shown that for a video of 4-5 minutes, fewer than 60% of your viewers will still be watching compared to 75% for a 1-2 minute video. On the other hand, you can invite people to an hour-long video and if you keep it lively and relevant, most people will stay. You can sprinkle multiple stories throughout.

Use Technology that's Most Comfortable for You

The most obvious type of video is a "talking head," in which people see you but there are other options. Examples are:

- Cartoons created with cartoon software
- PowerPoint slides (or slides created with Keynote, Google Slides, or other options)
- Screen captures, which are great for technical demos
- Later in this chapter, we'll suggest some tools you can use to create videos.

Use Images to Tell a Story

One simple image can be a powerful story. You've probably seen photojournalism that has made a lasting impression on you. Often these images are heartrending but joyful photos can also be highly impactful.

As we've mentioned, photos tend to have a more emotional effect because they're more realistic than an illustration. Nevertheless, sometimes you want to use an illustration, infographic, chart, map or diagram, especially in a more professional, business-like setting.

You can find legal images on stock photo sites – a number of them are free – and you can always take your own. You can then put them on slides that you use when you speak.

Tell Your Story When You Speak

Of course, you should incorporate your stories when you speak, whether in front of a live audience or online. Tell very short stories when you meet people at networking events—again, these can be live or online. A short customer story can make a great elevator speech.

Find the Right Tools to Convey Your Story

These days, everything seems more highly technical than when we just spoke out stories to people in the same room (or cave) as us.

Don't let a lack of resources, tools, or skills stop you from using the right medium. For example, many people think that video is hard, but as we've said, it's never been easier.

You can find tools and resources to make any kind of content creation easy, no matter what your skill level or budget.

Tools for Images

Here are some tools you can use to create and edit images and photos:

- **Fiverr:** This is a platform where you can find graphic designers (as well as editors, formatters, and more)
- **Canva:** Here you can create and edit photos and graphics
- **GIMP:** This is a free, open-source Photoshop clone.
- **Pixlr: This is a free photo editing website**
- **Snipping Tool:** This is Windows' screen capture tool. Use Grab if you're on a Mac
- **PowerPoint:** Many people don't realize that PowerPoint has powerful graphic editing capabilities
- **Your smartphone:** Obviously, you can take photos with your smartphone and there are many smartphone apps that let you edit them

Tools for Video

Here are some tools you can use to create and edit video:

- **iMovie (Mac) and Windows Movie Maker:** These are basic video editing tools
- **Camtasia:** This tool can do screen captures as well as powerful editing

- **PowerPoint:** You can export to video from PowerPoint using its animation tools or by just creating slides and setting the timing between slides.
- **Zoom:** This is video meeting software, but you can also share your screen. Just record to create a video.
- **Your webcam:** Your webcam has software that lets you create video
- **Your smartphone:** Yup, you can just use your smartphone. You might want to consider using a tripod to keep things steady. There are smartphone apps to help you edit and format video as well.

Live Events

The tools here help you create online live events—webinars and group meetings.

- GoToMeeting and GoToWebinar
- YouTube Live
- Zoom Meeting and Zoom Webinar
- Facebook Live
- ...and numerous others

Chapter Twenty-Four

Distribute Your Story

"Storytelling is our obligation to the next generation. Give something of meaning to your audience by inspiring, engaging, and educating them with story. Stop marketing. Start storytelling."
~ Laura Holloway

Where do you put your story? We've already referred to some of these options but it's worthwhile to delve deeper because the more places you put your story, the more people will see it.

Tell Your Story when You Speak

Obviously, you can – and should – tell your story or multiple stories – when you speak. Whether you're speaking in front of a live audience or online, in a formal situation or informally, you should include stories.

Tell Your Story in Your Book

Do you have a book? Many speakers use a book to show their expertise in a different format, to introduce people to what they do, or as a product that they sell.

You can put your origin story in your introduction or the first chapter to help people get to know you right away. You can add relevant stories throughout to keep readers interested and make your points more powerfully.

Tell Your Story on Your Website and Blog

You can tell stories on your website. Besides your blog, your About page is a great page for your origin story, customer stories, and product stories. You can tell a short version on your Home page.

Speaking about blog posts, think of ways to use stories often there. You'll engage people much more than with simple principles. Because blog posts are dated, you can easily use stories based on seasons, holidays, and current events.

Use Social Media to Tell Stories

Social media is a great place to tell stories. Again, seasonal material is appropriate. Tell stories about events in your life that relate to your business topic. I have a friend who is a business coach and almost every time she goes shopping, she has a lesson to tell about how the merchant did something right or wrong – and why. These personal/business stories are very effective.

Tell Stories in Emails

If you preface your emails with a very short story and relate it to what you're selling, you'll increase sales. That's because you'll draw your subscribers into the email with the story and elicit emotion from them. Think about how something you did or saw relates to the product you're selling and explicitly make the connection.

Here's an example from one of my recent emails:

"We're back in Davie, Florida and in 1-1/2 weeks, we'll be back in Iowa! I'm looking forward to seeing daffodils and tulips in my garden. Have you already seen signs of Spring?

Spring is an obvious symbol of growth and one of the best ways to grow your business is to grow your list. And one of the best ways to grow your list is to create multiple freebies to attract people to subscribe. More about that in a minute."

First, I talked about something personal and connected that to Spring. Then I connected Spring to growth. I connected plant growth to business growth. Then I connected business growth to the specific task of growing a subscriber list. Finally, I connected growing a subscriber list to the product I was offering on creating multiple free offers.

Post on Content Sites

You need to reach beyond your subscribers, followers, website visitors and one great way to do that is to post articles on content sites. Two sites that often don't get enough attention from online entrepreneurs are Medium.com and Reddit.com.

Medium is a place to publish articles. It gets millions of visitors each month and it's free to use although you can purchase an upgrade.

Reddit is a series of topic-based groups and there's one for almost everything. Reddit can get a little raw, but in most cases, people are helpful and supportive.

There are many other possibilities, including forums for trade/industry organizations.

Everything we've said about stories applies to articles. Either start with a short story or incorporate one into the article's content.

CHAPTER TWENTY-FIVE

Starting Your Stories

"Successful people maintain a positive focus in life no matter what is going on around them. They stay focused on their past successes rather than their past failures, and on the next action steps they need to take to get them closer to the fulfillment of their goals rather than all the other distractions that life presents to them."

~ Jack Canfield

Now you know...

- Why you need to use stories
- The 6 types of stories you can tell
- The 4 C's of story structure
- How to know which story is most effective for your market
- How to create a story that engages your readers
- How to know which media to use to create your story
- Where to distribute your story

Start with One Story and Let Them Multiply!

Now it's time to get to work on your story. Focus on just one story first. It may not be as perfect as you'd like if it's your first one, but you'll get better and better at storytelling the more you do it.

If you need help with the production side of things, you can always work with people who are experts in the skills that you lack.

Practice telling the story out loud and record yourself. Listen to the recording and you'll probably find something to tweak and improve. Then find as many places as possible to use it, in as many formats as you can.

Wishing you a happy ending!

PART V
What's Next?

"The only reason to give a speech is to change the world."
~ Nick Morgan

We have now painted a picture for you, in vivid color, as to what speaking is all about and how you can develop your public speaking to create an ongoing revenue stream. We (Ellen and Connie) have given you more than enough information and specific details for you to get started right away. Perhaps you have already begun, and simply need to make a few small tweaks and changes based on our recommendations in order to reach your full potential.

In our attempt to make this transition as easy and as simple as possible we have shown you how to can use this book as a template and blueprint for the "speaking to income" goals you wish to achieve. Think of these pages as a "dot to dot" outline where you decide which direction to go in next.

Think of this book also as a "choose your own adventure" guide for your future. Whether you are interested in speaking in person, virtually, or through online courses and trainings, the world is waiting for you to share your message and your essence. Speaker's speak, so the sooner you prepare to do this on a regular basis the sooner you will begin the transformation process.

You will also begin to see opportunities all around you that you may not have paid attention to in the past. Let everyone you know that you are available for speaking engagements on one or two topics. Perhaps one will be related to your business and the other more aligned with your mindset and perspective on life. Consider putting a "Speaking" page on your website listing your topics and including a short video from one of your talks.

Over the years I (Connie) have spoken on time management and productivity fairly often and even co-authored a book on this called *Time Management Strategies for Entrepreneurs: How to Manage Your Time to Increase Your Bottom Line* to give me additional credibility in this area.

As for me (Ellen), my most common topics for speaking have been presentation skills and making an income online. I've written a couple of e-books directed at speakers, such as *Quick and Dirty Podcast Profits Method, Slide Design for Non-Designers,* and *12 Steps to Become a Charismatic Speaker.*

As Dr. Seuss taught us, "Oh, the places you'll go" when you make the conscious decision to move forward in a way that serves your goals and your lifestyle. Speaking to create an ongoing stream of revenue is a worthwhile endeavor.

Just as readers are leaders, so are those who speak to share and empower and motivate and inspire. Step into your power as you stand tall and change the world.

If you want more guidance...

We would love the opportunity to connect with you and work further on your goals of turning your public speaking into an ongoing income stream. We have created specific resources for you that are targeted at newer and seasoned speakers alike. Opt in for these speaker resources at:

OnlineWritingProfits.com/speaker-resources

We also teach a course on the topic of this book. Information is at the above link.

Until we meet again, may your speaking open doors and allow you to live the life you want and deserve.

About the Authors

Ellen Finkelstein is an online entrepreneur, business coach, and presentation skills trainer. She started her career as a Teacher of the Transcendental Meditation Technique (which she still practices) and then was an Employee Benefits Manager before starting her own business.

As an author, she has written 11 published books (25 editions) for McGraw-Hill and Wiley and published 9 e-books during her 20-year career as an author. Her books have ranged from 20 pages to 1200+ pages.

Since 1999, Ellen has been helping people to present more effectively via her websites, EllenFinkelstein.com and OutstandingPresentationsWorkshop.com.

In that time, she learned a lot about Internet Marketing, which she teaches at ChangetheWorldMarketing.com. There she helps online entrepreneurs who want to make the world a better place and shows them how to reach audiences everywhere through writing and speaking—especially via webinars. She focuses on Internet marketing strategy and technology, making the complex easy, so marketers can actually take action and achieve their goals.

As an Adjunct Professor at Maharishi University of Management, Ellen has taught Web Writing, Creating a Usable Website, eBusiness, and Internet Marketing. She also provides Internet Marketing courses and coaching sessions.

You can find out more about Ellen at
ChangetheWorldMarketing.com/About

Connie Ragen Green is a bestselling author, international speaker, and online marketing strategist who is dedicating her life to serving others as they build and grow successful and lucrative online businesses. Her background includes working as a classroom teacher for twenty years, while simultaneously working in real estate. In 2006 she left it all behind to come online, and the rest is history.

She makes her home in two cities in southern California; Santa Clarita in the desert and Santa Barbara at the beach. In addition to her writing and work online, Connie consults and strategizes with several major corporations and some non-profits, as well as volunteering with groups such as the international service organization Rotary, the Boys & Girls Clubs, the Benevolent Protective Order of Elks, the women's business organization Zonta, and several other charitable groups.

As a recent recipient of the Merrill Hoffman Award, presented to Connie by the Santa Barbara Rotary Club, being honored with this award has strengthened her resolve to serve others around the world in any way she is able to by using her gifts, talents, and experiences in a positive and sincere manner.

Connie works with new entrepreneurs and authors on six continents to help them achieve their goals. If you want to create passive income streams, replace or supplement your current income, and get your message out to the world in the process, reach out to Connie and get started right away.

Find out more about Connie at

ConnieRagenGreen.com

www.ingramcontent.com/pod-product-compliance
Lightning Source LLC
LaVergne TN
LVHW010058110826
845155LV00028B/389

* 9 7 8 1 9 3 7 9 8 8 5 3 1 *